TRIAL

TRIAL
THE INSIDE STORY

SUSAN KUKLIN

HENRY HOLT AND COMPANY
NEW YORK

Henry Holt and Company, LLC
Publishers since 1866
115 West 18th Street
New York, New York 10011

Henry Holt is a registered trademark
of Henry Holt and Company, LLC

Published in Canada by Fitzhenry & Whiteside Ltd.,
195 Allstate Parkway, Markham, Ontario L3R 4T8.

Library of Congress Cataloging-in-Publication Data
Kuklin, Susan.
   Trial: the inside story / Susan Kuklin.
      p.   cm.
   Includes bibliographical references and index.
     1. Chen, Ren Jie—Trials, litigation, etc.—Juvenile literature.   2. Trials
(Kidnapping)—New York (N.Y.)—Juvenile literature.   3. Illegal aliens—
United States—Juvenile literature.   4. Smuggling—United States—
Juvenile literature.   [1. Chen, Ren Jie.   2. Trials (Kidnapping).
3. Kidnapping.   4. Illegal aliens.   5. Smuggling.]   I. Title.
   KF224.C39 K85 2000   345.73'0254—dc21   00-27783

ISBN 0-8050-6457-5
First Edition—2001
Printed in the United States of America on acid-free paper. ∞
10 9 8 7 6 5 4 3 2 1

CONTENTS

AUTHOR'S NOTE

This is a true story. It reports a criminal trial I followed from the day the jury was chosen until its very end. During the proceedings I interviewed both the judge and the defense attorney. To make certain that I would not impart confidential information to either side, I waited until after the verdict to talk to the prosecutor and the detectives who broke the case. The events that I did not personally witness were reconstructed from more than one thousand seven hundred pages of pretrial and trial transcripts, as well as from my own interviews.

. . .

The New York City District Attorney's office was concerned for the safety of the victims and the informants who were witnesses. They asked that I not reveal the names or locations of these individuals. I agreed to this request in advance.

The defense attorney's concern was that his client receive a fair trial. He would not allow me to interview the defendant because our conversations could subject me to being called as a witness by the prosecutor.

In fairness to the other Chinese participants whom I did not personally interview, I changed their names in order to respect their privacy.

. . .

Since I am not a lawyer, I wanted to be careful in describing the complexities of the criminal justice system. After I wrote the manuscript, I gave it to the judge, the prosecutor, and the defense attorney to check for accuracy. Then legal scholars and other lawyers read it as well. In spite of this help, mistakes may have slipped through the cracks. I plead guilty to any and all errors.

In order to make it easier to keep track of the legal issues and terminology used in the actual trial, I've put relevant explanations in boxes alongside the text and definitions in the glossary. When appropriate, I've repeated some explanations as reminders.

I am deeply grateful to Judge Bernard J. Fried, Assistant District Attorney Leemie Kahng, and Glenn Garber, defense attorney, for their time, candor, professionalism, and friendship. I could not have written this book without them.

My thanks to the following people who helped me along the way:

New York County District Attorney's office—
 Robert Morganthau, Jim Kindler, Caroline Basile;
Major Case Squad—
 David Chan, Hayman Goon;
Judge Fried's staff—
 Mary Cassidy, Elizabeth Candreva, Esq., Esther Josiah;
Brooklyn Law School—
 Professor Susan Herman, Professor Robert Pitler, Professor Tony Sebok, Sara Robbins, law librarian;

University of Connecticut Law School—

Professor Leonard Arland;

University of International Business and Economics (Beijing)—

Professor Wang Pei, Professor Jaio Jin Hong;

Friends and Family—

Refna Wilkin, Eliza Dresang, Nancy Machinton, Elizabeth Levy.

A special thanks to my editor, Marc Aronson, who took on a very lengthy, intricate manuscript and guided me through a number of drafts. Last, but hardly least, my husband, Bailey, who suggested that I write this book and then lived with it (and me) for the next two and a half years. He devoted countless hours reading drafts, asking probing questions, and teaching me the foundations of law. For his immeasurable love and encouragement, I dedicate this book to

Bailey H. Kuklin
and students of law,
past, present, and future

THE PLAYERS

BERNARD J. FRIED — presiding trial judge

LEEMIE KAHNG — assistant district attorney (the prosecutor)

GLENN GARBER — defense attorney

MARY CASSIDY — court clerk

DAVID CHAN — a New York detective from the Major Case Squad

HAYMAN GOON — a New York detective from the Major Case Squad

WANG DONG — the first victim, the complaining witness

LI JUN — the second victim, another complaining witness

JOE CHEN — the defendant

SONNY CHEN — his brother, already confessed to the crime

LUKE CHEN — his cousin, already confessed to the crime

JANE DING — his cousin in-law, already confessed to the crime and a cooperating witness

JOHNNY DING — a distant relative to Jane, already confessed to the crime and a cooperating witness

BUDDY PAN — a friend who was smuggled into America with Wang Dong

STICK — a person smuggled into America with Wang Dong

SUZY LING — Joe Chen's girlfriend

ECHO — Johnny Ding's girlfriend

PROCEDURE

I. A crime is committed.

II. The victim fills out a complaint report.

III. The investigation begins; law enforcement gathers evidence.

IV. Law enforcement arrests an alleged perpetrator.

V. The alleged perpetrator is arraigned.

VI. A bail hearing is held.

VII. The grand jury returns an indictment.

VIII. Discovery takes place in which documents and materials are gathered by both prosecutor and defender.

IX. Pretrial hearings are held to determine whether evidence should be suppressed.

X. The trial occurs.
   A. Jury selection.
   B. Opening statements.
      1. The prosecutor outlines the state's case.
      2. The defense attorney addresses the jury, if desired.

C. The prosecutor's case.
   1. Testimony of witnesses.
      a) Direct examination.
      b) Cross-examination.
      c) Redirect examination.
      d) Recross-examination.
      e) Redirect.
      f) Recross, etc.

D. The defense's case, if desired.
   1. Testimony of witnesses.
      a) Direct examination.
      b) Cross-examination.
      c) Redirect examination.
      d) Recross-examination.
      e) Redirect.
      f) Recross, etc.

E. Summations.

F. Judge's charge to the jury.

G. Jury deliberations.

H. The verdict.

If found guilty, the judge's sentence is pronounced. An appeal may be made to a higher court, the appellate court, to overturn the verdict or reduce the sentence.

CHRONOLOGY OF THE CASE

JULY 30, 1995, Wang Dong is kidnapped.

AUGUST 3, 1995, Li Jun is kidnapped.

AUGUST 13, 1995, both victims are released.

AUGUST 14, 1995, Mr. Wang calls "Crime Stoppers"; the complaint is
    forwarded to the Major Case Squad.

AUGUST 15, 1995, Mr. Wang meets with Detective Hayman Goon.

JULY 15, 1996, Jane Ding and Sonny Chen are arrested.

AUGUST 22, 1996, Luke Chen (Cow Eyes) is arrested.

APRIL 2, 1997, Leemie Kahng is assigned to prosecute the case.

MAY 8, 1997, Jane Ding, Sonny Chen, and Luke Chen plead guilty.

MAY 15, 1997, Jane Ding tells law enforcement that Johnny Ding is the leader
    of the kidnappers.

JUNE 20, 1997, Johnny Ding is arrested. He says that Joe Chen is the leader of
    the kidnappers. This is the first time law enforcement becomes aware of
    Joe Chen as a possible participant.

JUNE 24, 1997, Johnny Ding is the subject of a lineup before the two victims.

JUNE 30, 1997, Jane Ding makes another statement.

JULY 2, 1997, Detective David Chan arrests Joe Chen.

JULY 2, 1997, Joe Chen makes two statements to law enforcement.

JULY 5, 1997, Suzy Ling hires Glenn Garber to defend her boyfriend, Joe Chen.

FEBRUARY 11, 1998, the pretrial hearing is held before Judge Bernard J. Fried.

APRIL 14, 1998, the case goes to trial.

MAY 1, 1998, the verdict is reached.

TRIAL

MAY IT PLEASE THE COURT

- OPENING STATEMENTS: A BRUTAL DOUBLE KIDNAPPING HAS TAKEN PLACE.
- THE PROSECUTOR SETS THE SCENE AND DESCRIBES SOME OF THE EVIDENCE THAT SHE WILL BRING FORWARD DURING THE COURSE OF THE TRIAL.
- THE DEFENSE ATTORNEY GIVES HIS CLIENT'S VERSION OF THE KIDNAPPING OF THE TWO VICTIMS.
- THE JUDGE EXPLAINS THE LAW.

TIME: WEDNESDAY, APRIL 15, 1998; 9:30 A.M.
PLACE: STATE SUPREME COURT
111 CENTRE STREET, NEW YORK, N.Y., PART 75
THE HONORABLE BERNARD J. FRIED, PRESIDING

"May it please the court. My name is Leemie Kahng. I'm an assistant district attorney. I am here for the case of the People of the State of New York versus Joe Chen, the defendant, who is sitting right there." Boldly the young prosecutor whips her arm, forefinger pointed, toward a lanky young man who sits expressionless at the defense table. She pauses to let the moment sink in with the jury.

"Earlier, the judge told you that an opening statement is basically a preview of what is to come, as if you are watching a movie. This case is going to take you on a journey. It's going to take you on a journey into

Prosecutor Leemie Kahng and the map of China. (Her face is hidden at the request of the district attorney's office.)

an underground networked world that you may not be familiar with. This is the world of a group of Fujianese people. Let me explain who they are."

Leemie is dressed in a light-gray knit suit, very short skirt, white silk shirt, dark stockings, and black high heels. Her makeup subtly draws attention to heart-shaped lips. One might picture her a film-maker's ideal: beautiful, smart, aggressive. But make no mistake. Leemie Kahng is no actor. She is one hundred percent lawyer.

As the prosecutor, her job is to tell the story of a crime that will be confirmed by the evidence and the testimony of her witnesses. She faces the jury, twelve men and women of various ages and backgrounds, as well as four alternates, chosen in case one or more of the original twelve can no longer participate. The tension in the room does not make her job easy. She continues with her opening statement.

Leemie shows the jury a large map of China that sits on a stand in the "well" of the courtroom. The well, an area cordoned off from the public, is where all the business of the court takes place.

Bernard Fried is the presiding judge. He can't see the map from his raised desk, the bench. He interrupts the prosecutor to explain to the jury that the exhibit is not considered evidence. "I'm allowing it to be used only as demonstrative material to help you understand names."

The lawyer says, very, very respectfully, because she certainly doesn't want to alienate His Honor, "No, judge. This is the map of China."

"I'm sorry," he laughs. "The map is in evidence. I thought you were referring to the other one." To the jury he adds warmly, "You'll see what I'm talking about later. I won't interrupt you again." Everyone, with the exception of the defendant, smiles. Some jurors relax from the easy give-and-take between judge and lawyer.

The prosecutor uses the map to show where the people involved in this case are from in China, specifically, from Fujian Province.

"You are going to learn about a world of long boat rides, a world of smugglers—smugglers who are referred to as 'snake heads.' Snake heads arrange illegal trips from Fujian Province to America. It is a world that includes safe houses that snake heads have provided—"

"Objection," shouts Glenn Garber, the defense attorney.

"Overruled," the judge replies, and Leemie finishes her sentence.

"—when these smuggled aliens are brought into America. The safe houses are where the smugglers keep the individuals until their passage fare is paid.

"It is a world that you will probably find fascinating. It's also a world you will probably find very cruel.

"This case is about two victims, Mr. Wang Dong and Mr. Li Jun, who, as corny as it sounds, came here for the American dream. They came to pursue that dream, only to be betrayed by their fellow countrymen, only to be abducted and kidnapped and held for ransom by their fellow countrymen, and by *that* defendant who sits there." She glares at the defense table.

Another pause. Leemie softens the pitch of her voice to set the stage for going on to the plot. First she reads the indictments* (charges or accusations) against the defendant.

There are two counts of each charge because two different people, Mr. Wang and Mr. Li, were kidnapped.

---

* This and other legal terminology can be found in the glossary.

She moves on to the players in this entangled crime. Some of the kidnappers have already pleaded guilty and are serving time in prison. Leemie shows the jury a chart, the one the judge had referred to earlier, that shows the names of the people involved.

"Another participant in the kidnapping is the defendant's younger brother, Sonny Chen. Their cousin, Luke Chen, also took part in the crime," she says. "He is often referred to as—and this will probably be easier for you—Lew Mook. It's actually a nickname; it means 'Cow Eyes.'"

A third participant is a young woman whose name is Jane Ding.

Jane Ding is an in-law of the three Chens. Her husband is still in China. Later in the trial, Jane Ding will be a witness for the prosecution.

The jury will have a chart to keep track of the names and nicknames as the trial proceeds. The prosecutor continues.

"Another participant in the kidnapping is Johnny Ding. Sometimes he uses an alias. This will become important during the trial. He uses the name 'Charlie Chan.' He, too, will be a witness."

Johnny Ding, a.k.a. Charlie Chan, is a member of the vicious Tung On gang. He is a gangster. A kidnapper. A murderer. He is also a snake head who helped bring Sonny Chen, Jane Ding, and the first victim, Mr. Wang, to America.

The stage is set, and the main characters are identified. On to the plot. "These acquaintances are important in explaining how the two victims were brought to the defendant's apartment on Rivington Street. They will explain that the phone used to call the victims' families was in the defendant's name.

"And what you are going to hear is this: that the world of the victims and the world of the defendant brutally collided during the summer of 1995. You are going to hear from Mr. Wang, the first victim. He came to America on a boat with the defendant's younger brother, Sonny Chen, and their cousin-in-law, Jane Ding. There were maybe a hundred other aliens being smuggled on that boat. The boat ride lasted for months.

"The evidence is going to show that Jane Ding, Sonny Chen, Luke Chen—Cow Eyes—and the defendant sat in the defendant's apartment and planned the kidnapping. Because it was believed that Mr. Wang's family had money, the Chens suggested that Jane Ding call Mr. Wang and bring him to the apartment. When she called Mr. Wang, he agreed to meet her in Chinatown on July 30, 1995.

"Miss Ding then brought Mr. Wang to the apartment. Once inside, he saw the defendant's younger brother, Sonny Chen, and another person who *claimed* to be Johnny Ding, the man whose nickname is Charlie Chan. That's important, too, and I'm going to provide evidence about this later.

"Soon after being brought to the apartment, Mr. Wang was blindfolded, handcuffed, and beaten. You are going to hear evidence that the defendant took part in the beating, took part in trying to get the victim's phone number in China, and, eventually, succeeded in getting the number from Mr. Wang. Then they called Mr. Wang's relatives in China and demanded ransom money."

Leemie takes a deep breath and moves on to the second victim. "You are going to hear that on August 3 of 1995, Johnny Ding, who lived in another state at that time, ran into Mr. Li, the second victim, at the bus station in Baltimore.

"Johnny Ding suggested, 'Maybe you can come to my friend's apartment before you go to your immigration hearing in New York,' which was the next day.

"When they arrived in New York City, Johnny Ding called the apartment of Joe Chen and spoke to the defendant. Johnny Ding told him, 'I have a person that I just met on the bus. He doesn't know his way around New York.' The defendant said, 'We already have another person here. Why don't you bring him over.'" Both men were kidnapped.

After the victims' families in China paid the ransom, the prosecutor explains, the young men were released. They were warned not to report this crime to the police.

"But the witnesses did in fact call the police, and Sonny Chen, Jane Ding, and Cow Eyes were apprehended."

Now that the basic story line is laid out, the assistant district attorney describes how she will proceed with the trial. "Besides the victims themselves, you are going to hear the testimonies of Jane and Johnny Ding, as well as the detectives who took part in the arrests, and a Bell Atlantic telephone investigator. The collection of all their testimonies, and all of the evidence in the case, will prove the defendant is guilty beyond a reasonable doubt."

Throughout this opening statement, Leemie Kahng stands in the middle of the well of the court. Now she walks directly to the jurors. "You promised and you assured this court that you would keep an open mind. I'm going to ask you at the conclusion of the case—after the evidence has been presented against this defendant, Joe Chen—I'm going to ask you to come back with the only verdict possible: guilty on all charges and all counts. Thank you." The prosecutor quickly takes her seat.

Judge Fried asks, "Mr. Garber, do you care to give an opening statement?"

The defense does not have to make an opening statement. He

doesn't have to prove his client is innocent. He doesn't have to prove that his client is a nice guy. He doesn't even have to offer any evidence. He simply has to show that the prosecutor has not proved her case beyond a reasonable doubt. The burden of proof is always on the prosecutor. It never shifts to the defense.

But Glenn Garber will address the jury. He wants them to know his client's version of the events before they hear the prosecutor's evidence.

"Yes, Your Honor," he says. "Thank you." He walks to the jury box.

"Good morning, ladies and gentlemen." A few jurors nod back at him, a bit self-consciously.

Glenn is a good-looking, easygoing fellow, about the same age as the prosecutor. He has a friendly smile and shiny hazel eyes. But in court Glenn is a fierce defender who will fight tooth and nail on behalf of his client. In court he wears business clothing.

When he is away from the courtroom, his uniform of choice is a pair of faded jeans, a T-shirt, and an old wrinkled shirt. Today he is in his blue pinstriped suit, starched white dress shirt, and maroon-and-navy paisley tie.

"Joe Chen was present in that apartment at certain times, and he knew a little bit about the kidnapping," he tells the jury. "The actors are related. They are a family. That is why Joe Chen was there. But the case is about whether or not the prosecutor proves beyond a reasonable

Defense attorney Glenn Garber.

doubt that Joe Chen actually participated in this particular kidnapping. I submit that she will not prove that.

"Joe Chen sublet his apartment to his brother. My client was not even living there. Jane Ding convinced Sonny Chen to assist her in a kidnapping. Johnny Ding, the gangster you heard about earlier, is distantly related to Jane Ding. He is actually the leader and orchestrator of this kidnapping.

"Johnny Ding is a convicted murderer. He also has been given a deal by the government to cooperate against this defendant.

"After the investigation revealed that the defendant's name was attached to the apartment, and that the phone was in his name, things twisted. To save his own hide, Johnny Ding, who is actually the leader of this kidnapping, falsely accused my client.

"I submit to you, ladies and gentlemen, that the accusations that the defendant assumed some sort of leadership role, or participated in those kidnappings, are false. The prosecutor will not prove beyond a reasonable doubt that Joe Chen is guilty of the kidnappings. Thank you very much." Glenn Garber takes his seat, leans over, and places his arm around his client's shoulders.

.   .   .

Throughout the three-week trial, this writer sits in the gallery behind Joe Chen. Every morning, handcuffed and surrounded by guards, he arrives in court before the jury is brought in. Joe must be present with a translator at all proceedings concerning his case. "Good morning," he mouths. I return his greeting. It is hard to imagine that this shy, spike-haired twenty-seven-year-old in a slightly oversized gray suit could be a heartless kidnapper.

Sometimes court personnel pay brief visits to the proceedings.

Other times a journalist from a local Chinese newspaper is there. Occasionally there are groups of teenagers on school trips. But most days I am the only nonparticipant in the courtroom. Neither friends nor family visit Joe Chen throughout the proceedings.

Like the two victims, Joe is an illegal alien. But because the crime took place on American soil, this fact plays no role in the trial. Both the victims and the defendant are entitled to the same protection, and must obey the same rules, as any citizen in this country.

Everyone connected to this trial has at least one foot in the door of another country. Either they themselves are immigrants or they are the children of immigrants. Collectively they come from Romania, Korea, Russia, Poland, Austria, China, Cuba, Italy, and Ireland. This then is a trial for immigrants (the victims), of an immigrant (the defendant), and by immigrants (everyone else). And yet the fact that they are immigrants, legal or illegal, plays no role in the proceedings. What unites them—and you and me—is a system of laws that governs every one of us.

In between courtroom sessions, some mornings, and during many lunch breaks, Judge Bernard Fried explains to me what is happening, legally, in court. Because it is inappropriate to tape conversations in the courthouse, we often have these lessons in various Asian restaurants in Chinatown, the neighborhood adjacent to the courts in downtown Manhattan. He will not give his personal opinion about this trial; he speaks only in general terms.

The judge explains that Leemie Kahng and Glenn Garber have two very different objectives. The prosecutor begins with an outline of the evidence that she plans to offer during the course of the trial. Her overall objective is to represent the interests of the state. Her primary task is to present evidence to support the charges.

The defense attorney is to represent his client with zeal. To do so, he will use every legal avenue available to him to make sure the client is properly defended. This includes an important job: to keep the state—and all the evidence the state produces—fair and honest.

The lawyers for each side are to make the best case they can, within the rules of the law. The judge interprets the rules and acts as a referee for the two lawyers. The jury applies the law to the evidence to determine whether the prosecutor has made a sufficient case.

. . .

After the lunch break, the jurors are brought back to the courtroom. There is no doubt that a brutal double kidnapping has taken place. Was Joe Chen the leader of the kidnappers? Or did he merely sublet his apartment and lend his telephone to the wrong relatives at the wrong time?

"Are you ready to call your first witness?" asks Judge Fried, peering over his glasses at the prosecutor. "Yes," she replies. "The People call Mr. Wang."

. . .

Mr. Wang waits outside the courtroom. He is here to tell the jury about the chain of events that changed his life forever. It began early one morning on a dock in Fuzhou, China. It began with the snake heads....

# COMING TO AMERICA

• WANG DONG DESCRIBES HOW HE WAS SMUGGLED TO AMERICA. AND MORE.

DATE: SPRING 1994
PLACE: A DOCK IN FUZHOU, CHINA

The sky begins to lighten with the coming of dawn, and a thick blanket of fog covers the waterfront. Finally, out of the gray, a man appears. He is a snake head.

Mr. Wang and his best friend, Buddy Pan, join twenty other young people who crowd into a small speedboat that races out to sea. A mile or so out, they are transferred to a larger ship carrying about two hundred young people. The boys are sent to dormitory-style bunks in the lower level of the ship. The girls, many fewer in number, are given rooms upstairs.

Wang and his friend are following the footsteps of generation upon generation of Fujianese seafarers who, since the time of the

A street in China similar to the neighborhood in which Mr. Wang grew up.

Qin dynasty, have immigrated to such far-off lands as Indonesia, Malaysia, Singapore, and the Philippines.

In the beginning Mr. Wang is seasick. He says, "I was so dizzy. I ate a little and went to sleep. Then I got used to it. I'd play cards or chess, hang around, and talk about funny things."

Also on the boat are Sonny Chen and his cousin's wife, Jane Ding. Mr. Wang is assigned to a bunk next to Sonny. "Being together for so long a period of time, naturally we got to know each other," Mr. Wang says. Along with Mr. Wang's friend, Buddy Pan, and another man, a skinny kid called Stick, they form a clique and take their meals together.

"We listened to the snake head. He arranged our meals. He gave us weather reports. He took care of arguments. He maintained the order and safety of the ship."

Long, dull days become boring, uneventful months as the ship zigzags across the Pacific, dodging government ships and luxury liners. At last, day seventy-two to be exact, Mr. Wang looks out at the never-ending seascape. Far, far off in the horizon he sees something new: land. Quickly he finds his friends to tell them.

In no time the fivesome bundle their meager possessions into their backpacks and line up with the others. As at the beginning of their voyage, they are transferred to smaller boats. These take them to a place called Mexico.

The group of about two hundred young people arrives safely and is divided into two teams. Mr. Wang says, "The second team wasn't that healthy or they were female. The snake head transferred us by car to a safe house, where we were fed a meal and took showers, our first hot showers. I was in the stronger physical team, the first team." Although she is female, Jane Ding opts to stay with her buddies in the first team. Mr. Wang, Buddy, Sonny, Stick, and Jane begin a long trek over a mountain to their destination. "After climbing the mountain I was in the U.S.A."

After the snake head makes a phone call, a new man arrives in a van to drive them to another safe house in Los Angeles. "The houses were very pretty. It seems to me it was a high-class place. Actually, where that place was, I have no idea."

Later, yet another snake head arrives and drives them to the Los Angeles airport. "The person who represented us bought our air tickets and then showed us how to get on the plane. When we arrived, new snake heads met us and took us to a new safe house somewhere in New York State.

"We were in this place where all the windows were covered by cloth. Day and night there were two people watching us. They would not permit any of us to have freedom of movement. When it was time to eat, we were called to have our meal. Afterwards, we were told to stay on the floor where our beds were."

Mr. Wang and his fellow captives remain at the safe house until their families back in China pay the smuggler's fee. Wang says, "It made sense to hold us there." The smugglers want money; they are not doing this for charity. "The first day after I got there, the snake head gave me a telephone to call my sister." Wang's family quickly pulled together their life savings and borrowed extra from friends to pay the smuggler's fee. "Approximately two days later I made another call to my family, who said that the money was ready." Mr. Wang's fee is $26,000.

Mr. Wang's friends are not as lucky. They remain in the safe house longer, while their families hustle to come up with the cash. They comment to one another that Mr. Wang must come from a rich family.

Meanwhile, Mr. Wang is driven to a restaurant in New York City's Chinatown where his niece is waiting for him. He is free.

"My niece owns a restaurant in another city. I lived with her and her boyfriend and some employees. I worked there for one year. I had a debt to pay. I owed my family $26,000. I paid back the full amount. I worked so hard and gradually saved from my job."

ONE YEAR LATER: JULY 1995

"Do you know who I am?" Jane Ding asks her friend from the smuggler's ship. Mr. Wang, who is still working in his niece's restaurant, is not sure who is on the telephone.

"It is Jane Ding," she says with a nervous laugh, trying her best to sound casual.

"How did you get my number?" he asks, surprised but not unhappy.

"Your friend Buddy gave it to me." Jane wants to see her traveling companion again. Perhaps they can meet on his day off? Mr. Wang is delighted.

They arrange to have tea in New York City the following Sunday. On the Friday before their reunion, she calls again, just to be sure he is coming.

"Of course. I'll come at eight A.M." Though a bit puzzled by the call, he goes back to work at the restaurant and never gives her inquiry a second thought.

On Sunday, when Mr. Wang goes to the bus station, he learns that there are no buses until noon. Since he does not have Jane's telephone number, he waits at the station, hoping she does not give up and leave.

"When I arrived, she was waiting for me. When she saw me, she was quite happy to see me." Jane asked why he was so late. He apologized and explained the mixup.

Mr. Wang and Jane go to a small restaurant for a bite to eat. When they finish, Jane suggests a walk through Chinatown. They stroll a few blocks and find themselves in front of an apartment building. Without so much as an explanation, Jane takes out a key, opens the door, and invites him inside. "I walked in. She was right behind me.

"We went downstairs to an apartment. After I entered the room, I saw two persons sitting by the table." Jane slams the door shut and runs into another room. "The two individuals were Sonny Chen, who came over with me, and someone I didn't know." Things began to happen. Fast. So fast he could hardly react.

"Sonny Chen tapped my shoulder and told me to go into another room. The other person came by my side. He had a knife. I was told to sit by the side of the bed. Then someone got handcuffs, and a red cloth was put over my eyes."

DATE: MAY 1998
PLACE: THE DISTRICT ATTORNEY'S OFFICE

Leemie Kahng, ever tidy, scoops up a piece of crumpled paper from the floor as she walks briskly to her windowless office. "It may sound corny," she tells me, "but I'm so proud of this office. I believe it stands for truth and justice." Leemie's family are an ideal example of the American dream that she talked about in her opening statement. They immigrated from Korea when Leemie was three. They worked hard, became successful, and sent their two daughters to fine schools. Leemie says, "For my parents to come here, and for me to be where I am, I think America is pretty great."

Tossing the crumpled paper into a wastebasket, Leemie puts down her briefcase. We talk about the case she has just finished—a double kidnapping.

The families of Mr. Wang and another man, Mr. Li, paid big ransoms for the release of their sons. Now they wanted justice.

Leemie has heard this before. In recent years there has been a rash of kidnappings in Chinatown. Although the kidnappers are often caught, their cases rarely go to trial. More likely than not, the complaining witnesses, people like Mr. Wang and Mr. Li, never show up in court to testify.

Most victims do not know their legal rights. They do not speak English. They are afraid of retribution against either themselves or their families back in China. They are afraid they will be deported. And so they become no-shows. Without a victim's testimony there is no case. She expected the same from these two men.

She was wrong.

Once Leemie realized that Mr. Wang would press charges, she knew she had a very big case on her hands. Her first big case. "I felt a heavy burden and a social responsibility to the Chinese community. I felt a responsibility to my victims and to their families. The whole thing was very nerve-racking."

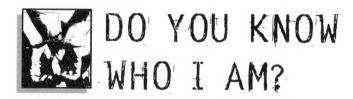

DO YOU KNOW WHO I AM?

- PROSECUTOR LEEMIE KAHNG CALLS THE FIRST VICTIM TO THE STAND.
- MR. WANG DESCRIBES THE KIDNAPPING.

DATE: WEDNESDAY, APRIL 15, 1998; 2:30 P.M.
PLACE: JUDGE FRIED'S COURTROOM

"At this time the People call Mr. Wang."

Mr. Wang is the first victim. Leemie says that some judges do not like the prosecutor to use the word "victim" because it invokes too much sympathy. Evidence, not sympathy, is to decide the case. "I try to call them 'complaining witnesses' in all my cases."

· · ·

A husky young man in a pale-blue button-down shirt, denim jacket, and jeans enters the courtroom. In a wink he leaps into the witness box, whirls around, and scrutinizes the defendant, as if to ask, "Is this the man who did bad things to me?" He quickly composes himself and sits down beside the court translator, a young woman who is also from Fujian Province.

THE COMPLAINING WITNESS:
The victim.

Leemie explains why she put Mr. Wang on the stand first. "I want the jury to understand Wang Dong as a human being." This task will not be easy because everything must be communicated through a translator. Unlike dramatic courtroom shows in the movies or on TV, the process of questioning a witness is slow and repetitive.

Mary Cassidy, the court clerk, asks the witness to take an oath. Mr. Wang doesn't understand why he needs to place his hand on the Bible. The interpreter explains this procedure several times in two dialects, first in Fujianese and then in Mandarin. His hand trembles as it rests on the Bible.

Judge Fried asks a second interpreter, sitting next to Joe Chen, to explain to the defendant that if he has trouble understanding the person speaking, he should raise his hand. Joe Chen responds with a nod.

With the help of Leemie's questions, Mr. Wang tells the jury that he was born in Fujian, China, in 1968. After he graduated from high school, he became a driver. He describes his voyage to America and his fateful friendship with Sonny Chen and Jane Ding. Then he talks about the kidnapping:

Let me try to remember the details. I was handcuffed and blindfolded. The guy with the knife asked, "Do you know who I am?" I said I did not. He said—he said, "I am that person called Johnny Ding."

After that, he and Sonny started beating me for about ten minutes. They used their fists to beat me up. They hit me over here and over here, on the upper part of my body. They hit me over here, over here, over here on my shoulders and back.

After the beating they changed the positioning of my handcuffs and cuffed me to a window grate. And that's how I was kept there. Someone stayed in the room night and day. Quite a few people came in, about five or more, and a phone was brought in. I remained blindfolded with a red cloth. When I moved my eyelids around, the fabric moved and I could see a little.

They made me give them my family's phone number. My niece from upstate just happened to be in China. She picked up the phone. As soon as I got on the phone, I told my family that I had been kidnapped. During that time they continued to hit me.

They took the phone and said, "We caught your family member. You must get $20,000 ready immediately. I will give you a beeper number in China. As soon as you get the money ready, call that beeper and give the money to that person." If not, they will get rid of me.

During the conversation they continued to beat me so my family will hear. After that they locked me to the window grate and nothing else happened that night. My right arm was up into the air and I was in a kneeling position all day.

The next day Sonny Chen stayed with me. I told him to lower my arm. He lowered my arm. I lay down on the floor because I was really, really tired. I was still blindfolded.

At least three days later, Sonny Chen came and locked me back in a high position. About an hour after that there was another person kidnapped by them. They unlocked me and took me to another room and locked me to the bed.

After that I was locked in that other room. Somebody hit me three times, here, really hard. He told me that the other person had just been kidnapped. His finger—one of his fingers was already been cut off. And he waved it in front of me.

He asked me, "Do you want me to take off your cloth and let you see?" I said, "No."

After that he brought me to the original room and put me together with that person who had just been kidnapped. His hand was handcuffed to the window and I was handcuffed to him. Every once in a while someone *came in and hit us. Later I learned who this person was, the individual named Li.*

When there's nobody else in the room, Li talked to me. He said, "After we are released from here, we should contact each other." He told me his name and phone number.

Me and Mr. Li were always beaten by somebody. Mr. Li was hit more often than I was. Sonny Chen had a gun. Someone else had a gun, too, but I could not determine who it was.

We didn't have much food to eat. We shared one instant noodle soup a day.

I contacted my family three or four times with a cellular phone. During the calls they sometimes hit me and asked me to tell my family to get the money as fast as possible.

My family member begged them, "Please. We cannot gather twenty thousand dollars. We are able to get fifteen thousand." They did lower the amount to fifteen thousand. My family gave the money to the people in China. After I was released, I called my family.

Leemie stops the description and says, "Judge, at this time can I have People's Exhibits marked for identification?"

"Read them into the record."

Until a document or a photograph is received in evidence, the jury cannot look at it. Remember, the trial's purpose is not only to determine whether the defendant is guilty beyond a reasonable doubt, but also to make sure this determination satisfies other purposes of the trial, including that the government has properly obtained evidence. Judge Fried explains that a reason for this formal procedure is to help ensure that there is no improper evidence admitted.

JUDGE FRIED SAYS:

Before the court can receive a document into evidence, a *foundation* must be laid:

1. The document has to be authentic.
2. The document has to be relevant.
3. The document has to be identified by the witness.

Leemie quickly reads the labeled photographs into evidence: "Can I have 2F as in Frank, 2J, 2K, and 2P as in Peter shown to the witness?"

From the photographs the witness identifies the interiors of the apartment, the kitchen, the halls, the bathroom, the stairs going down to the basement, and the metal grate where he had been handcuffed. These photographs, now marked as evidence, are given to the jury to look at more closely.

"Mr. Wang," questions Leemie, "you said that you were held in this apartment for about two weeks?"

"That's right."

"Can you describe the circumstances of your release?"

On the day I was to leave there were two persons with me and Mr. Li. One said, "You can take off your blindfold and leave the place, but you must walk with your head down for five or six blocks. Later you can look

around. If we realize that you turned around, we have a gun and we will shoot you."

And then they, the two persons, they walked out of the house. Later me and Mr. Li took off the blindfold and we walked very fast looking down. After we walked a distance, I saw a subway station and I got into the subway.

Evidence photo: Kitchen where the kidnap victims were held.

Mr. Li said he had to go to his relatives, his family's place in another state. I took the subway to 42nd Street. I had a ticket that allowed me to

Evidence photo: Front of the apartment where the victims were held.

go to my relatives' place. The following day I called the police and reported the case. Later I gave the police Mr. Li's telephone number.

Leemie asks the judge if she can stop at this point. He smiles, "I don't believe the jurors will have an objection to that. We will resume tomorrow morning at nine-thirty. Please don't discuss the case among yourselves. Have a pleasant evening."

The jury leaves for the day, but the lawyers are not finished. During the course of the trial, the lawyers work with Judge Fried on legal issues concerning both current and future witnesses. The defense attorney has the right to receive all the materials relating to the witnesses that the prosecution will be using against his client. (In New York this is called Rosario.) Sometimes the evidence will be judged inadmissible, that is, not allowed to be brought before the jury. One of a judge's responsibilities is to determine what can and what cannot be told to the jury. Rulings from previous cases, case law, are the basis for his decisions. For example, evidence may be inadmissible because it is irrelevant or inflammatory.

Throughout the trial the lawyers will try to predict each other's strategies. "It sounds difficult," Leemie explains, "but it's not as hard as one might

> **JUDGE FRIED SAYS:**
> The Rosario decision (in federal courts it is known as the Jenks Act) holds that a defendant is entitled to be given all pretrial statements that relate to a witness's testimony at the trial.
>
> This rule allows the defense to have a more meaningful cross-examination. The defense attorney can use this information to search for inconsistencies in prior statements, to test the memory of the witness, and to attack the credibility of a witness.

think. Once you've done it long enough, you can recognize how an examination will go. I know in advance what the defense is going to highlight. And he knows what my evidence is.

"Besides, in the courtroom everything is so elevated. My senses are elevated, every part of my being is on alert."

.   .   .

Defense attorney Glenn Garber asks to approach the side of the bench where he, Leemie, Mary Cassidy, and Judge Fried make up a human square. Linda Friedberg, the court stenographer, sits in the middle with a portable steno machine, keeping a record of their conversation. Although these planning discussions are on the record, the jury may not hear them because they are not evidence.

The prosecutor has a file that Glenn wants to examine. The file is about a different kidnapping. Sonny Chen, the defendant's brother, was the victim in that kidnapping. The kidnappers were caught, but the case never went to trial because Sonny would not come forward and identify them. Now Glenn wants to see all the files about this incident. He is looking for information that will protect his client.

Evidence photo: The grate where Mr. Wang and Mr. Li were handcuffed.

.   .   .

Leemie does not want to give Glenn the file. One, she believes that it is not relevant. Two,

Evidence photo: The bedroom where the kidnapping took place.

it could muddy the issues by taking the focus away from this kidnapping. "I have told him that there's really nothing relevant for this proceeding in those files," Leemie politely tells the judge.

"Is the brother a potential witness for the defense?" Judge Fried asks.

"Yes," says Glenn.

"In that case, you may proceed with your argument."

Glenn explains why he wants the files. "It is my understanding that my client was the person who reported this kidnapping to the police. The fact that my client reported that kidnapping, and the fact that his brother was held in captivity for a period of time, is relevant."

"What's the relevance?" asks the judge.

"The fact that he would turn against other kidnappers, report a crime to the police, and act as an ally to the police."

"I still don't understand the relevance," says the judge.

"I think the jury—"

The judge interrupts. "Are you suggesting that the fact that your client once reported a kidnapping crime is somehow a defense in this case? Is that what you mean?"

Glenn tries to explain. "It diminishes my client's supposed position as the leader of a gang, which Ms. Kahng is going to present later in this case. That's why it is relevant."

Though the judge appears not to agree with

RELEVANT:
Evidence or testimony that tends to support the case in a direct way is considered relevant and is admissible during the trial.

Glenn's reasoning, he holds off making this decision until later, when the brother testifies for the defense.

"Anything else?" asks the judge.

Leemie pipes up, "I don't want to cut into Mr. Garber's time, but there is one outstanding issue: the phone bills." Glenn wants revealed the names and telephone numbers that the victims gave the kidnappers. Leemie is worried for the safety of the victims and their families. She does not want their phone numbers released into the public record. She wants the numbers to be redacted—blacked out from the records.

Glenn wants every shred of evidence in advance to look for ways to best defend his client. Both arguments seem fair. A trial, though, is not about what seems fair on the surface; it is about how fairness is defined under the rules of law. Each side has to keep abreast of these rules. And each side will seek to interpret the rules to its own advantage.

"Do you have authority for redacting them?" the judge asks her.

At this point she does not, but she wants one night to research the case law to support her position.

The proceedings are adjourned. Joe Chen is handcuffed and escorted out of the courtroom by three armed guards.

· · ·

Leemie rushes back to her office to confer with her supervisor. "Because this is the first time I am trying a case of this magnitude, I want to be very, very cautious," she later tells me.

The supervisor believes that because the names and telephone numbers are evidence, Leemie cannot hold them back. "I stayed up all night looking up case law that will back up my argument. Most of my research was finished before the trial began, but I didn't anticipate this issue as being a problem."

Searching case law takes time. There are thousands of pages of previous court cases to read, and this trial, like a moving train, will not stop.

Meanwhile, Glenn is convinced that Leemie is deliberately stonewalling him. He's entitled to see all the evidence. He knows that *she* knows that as well.

Glenn returns to his office, which is chockablock with files and law books. There are still witnesses to talk to and questions to compose. Glenn must analyze every document and every police interview that the state plans to use in the trial. Remember, an important role of the defense attorney is to make certain that the state does not overreach with improperly obtained evidence. It's a lot of material, and Glenn's train won't stop either.

Glenn calls his wife in New Jersey: "Don't wait up. I'll just grab a sandwich here."

# I CANNOT
BE CERTAIN

- Leemie continues her direct examination of Mr. Wang.
- Glenn cross-examines the victim.

TIME: THURSDAY, APRIL 16, 1998; 9:00 A.M.
PLACE: OUTSIDE THE COURTHOUSE

His Honor Bernard Fried kisses his wife good-bye—"Have a nice day"—when she drops him off at the judge's entrance to the court-house. He watches as she drives off, heading south toward Brooklyn and the federal courts where she is a judge.

He uses a plastic card to open the JUDGES ONLY elevator. It seems that everyone else in the lobby floods in with him. Judges. Police officers. Guards. Clerks. Secretaries. "Good mornings" all around.

Arriving in chambers, the judge greets his law clerk, Elizabeth Candreva, and his secretary, Esther Josiah, who are already working. He takes off his sport coat and hangs it beside one of two black judge's robes. He looks at his computer. The screen saver has a photograph of his grandchild. He smiles as if she was there and taps a key two times to

Judge Fried in his chambers.

bring up his calendar. He dunks a Lapsang souchong tea bag into a mug of boiling water. "Anyone want tea?" he calls to his staff. "Coffee?"

"Nope, we've already had," they reply.

Bernard Fried has been a trial judge for eighteen years. "My job is very, very interesting," he says. "I love my job."

The telephone rings. It's Mother Superior. "Good morning, judge. Ten o'clock and all are present."

MOTHER SUPERIOR

A large bowl of candy and a box of tissues sit on Mary Cassidy's desk inside the well of the courtroom. Mary is referred to as Mother Superior by just about everyone in the building. She is Judge Fried's court clerk. She watches over the judge's courtroom like a robin protecting her chicks, keeping account of the witnesses, recording the exhibits into a ledger, and administering oaths to the witnesses. Mary says, "I tell people this is the best job I have ever had. It fulfills my life-long addiction to murder mysteries."

After Mary telephones the judge, he puts on his robe, takes one last sip of tea, and sprints up the back stairwell to his courtroom. With everyone in place, a guard escorts the jury into the courtroom and the witness returns to the stand.

When Judge Fried asks the lawyers to continue, Leemie thanks the judge and approaches the witness box. Mary reminds the witness that he is still under oath. Mr. Wang appears less nervous.

Mr. Wang explains that after his first beating, "Sonny Chen lay on the bed and I was handcuffed to the bar. I chatted with him. He said it was under somebody else's order that I was kidnapped."

The prosecutor asks, "After Jane Ding brought you into the apartment, did you have any other contact with her during that whole period of time that you were in the apartment?"

"I had no contact with her."

"Did she say anything to you after you were brought into the apartment?"

"Objection!" shouts Glenn, anticipating Leemie's future questions. Glenn supposes that Leemie is trying to get the witness to repeat what somebody else has said about the defendant. That is hearsay and not admissible.

"Can we go to the side, please," the judge says. Away from the ears of the jurors, the judge asks what the objection is. "She's started to lay a foundation for hearsay," Glenn replies. Glenn's voice is calm and professional, but his face reddens ever so slightly.

> **HEARSAY EVIDENCE:**
> The witness cannot repeat conversations that he or she heard about from a third party, with certain exceptions.

Leemie says that she is not. "I'm trying to elicit that *she* didn't say anything to him, *she* didn't do anything to him." It is not hearsay. They return to open court. "The objection is overruled," the judge says. Leemie can ask this question.

The prosecutor continues her questioning. "Did Jane Ding ever say anything to *you* during the time you were in the apartment?"

"No."

"Did she do anything to *you* while you were in the apartment?"

"No."

"Did you ever hear her give orders to anybody concerning *you* while you were in the apartment?"

"No."

Glenn, annoyed by Leemie's pointed emphasis of the word *you,* clenches his pencil but remains silent.

Moving to a new issue, Leemie asks, "Do you know a person by the name Stick?"

"He was on the boat with me." One day, while Mr. Wang was held captive, someone beat him severely on the upper chest. He thinks he heard Stick's voice say, "Do not hit him." He's not sure though. "I never heard Stick's voice after that day." Then he adds, "Afterwards, there was another person who said Mr. Li's finger has been chopped off. That person, I realized, was often there. He carried a cell phone all the time, and he could speak a little English."

Leemie has two objectives: one, to elicit more details of Mr. Wang's life in captivity, and two, to establish that the man whose voice he heard, the man with the cell phone, could only be Joe Chen. She moves closer to the witness. "So other than Sonny Chen, Jane Ding, and Stick, did you personally know anybody who was in the apartment during that period of time?"

Eyes like Cow. Cow Eyes. That's a nickname, I'm pretty sure. That's what other people always called him. Cow Eyes sometimes hit me. He punched me and my arm went numb. At night Sonny Chen slept in the bed while Cow Eyes slept across the door, across the doorway, to block the doorway.

The apartment lights were always on. The cloth over my eyes often became loose. Sometimes I could see through the cloth. I could see Sonny Chen and the person known as Cow Eyes. I couldn't exactly see their faces but he, Cow Eyes, was taller than Sonny Chen.

In the beginning my hand was cuffed very tight and was hurting. I asked Sonny whether he can loosen up a little. He agreed to my request. And on one night, one night I was able to loosen myself from the hand-

cuffs. Sonny was already asleep. I took the blindfold off. I slowly went to the door of the room and went out.

As soon as I got outside, I was able to see in the kitchen. There was a table in the kitchen with four sides and a lot of people around it. I was very scared so I went back to my original position. After I got inside, I quickly put my blindfold on and put my hands into the handcuffs. Sonny jumped up and asked, "What are you doing?" I said, "Nothing."

I didn't have a chance to see the faces of the people around the table. As soon as I saw that there were people, I returned right away.

Sonny told me not to move. "If you move," he said, "people outside will beat you to death."

During that period of time, I tried to speak with Sonny. I said, "Sonny Chen, we came to this country in the same ship. During that trip we took in a lot of hard time. That's very difficult for us to come here. Now you kidnapped me? It's really not a good thing to do." He said he's only following somebody's order and he has no choice.

I asked him whether he can reduce the amount of money they are asking for. He said, "I will try to help you and I'll try to talk to the group about the money."

WHO IS JOHNNY DING?

Here comes a tricky section in the trial. Mr. Wang says that one of the kidnappers said that his name was Johnny Ding. A few days later a second victim is brought to the apartment by a man called Charlie Chan. Charlie Chan is Johnny Ding's nickname.

Mr. Wang is certain that the man he first heard and the man who kidnapped the other victim are two different people. Who then was the first Johnny Ding?

Leemie implies that that person is the defendant, using the name Johnny Ding to hide his own identity. Glenn will later suggest that per-

LEEMIE KAHNG'S CHART:

Joe Chen—the defendant
Sonny Chen—his brother
Luke Chen—his cousin, also known as "Cow Eyes"
Jane Ding—cousin by marriage
Johnny Ding—a distant cousin of Jane Ding, also known as "Charlie Chan"

son could be one of any number of people, some of whom are still at large.

The jury looks at Leemie Kahng's name chart to reduce the confusion. Leemie needs another identification to reinforce her argument.

Mr. Wang tells the jury that the man with the cell phone—the first Johnny Ding—was often accompanied by a woman with very long hair. Although this woman never spoke to Mr. Wang, he figures that she was the first Johnny Ding's girlfriend.

But then, after the second victim was brought to the apartment, yet another woman arrived. She came with the real Johnny Ding, a.k.a. Charlie Chan.

Mr. Wang says that the second woman was very kind.

She brought me food, an apple. I deeply appreciated what she was doing. I told her—I said in Mandarin—I said, "Female usually has a heart like a mother." And she replied to me, saying, "Of course."

I cannot describe this woman.

Leemie asks, "Mr. Wang, can you tell me whether anybody here in this courtroom was at the apartment during that period of time?" He stares at everyone: the jurors, lawyers, Mother Superior, the guards, and even the judge. He studies Joe Chen's face for a long time. Finally, head lowered, his voice is barely a whisper. "I cannot be certain."

Glenn Garber scribbles his response on a yellow legal pad and underlines it two times. *"I cannot be certain!"*

. . .

Although Leemie cannot tell how the jury is responding, she believes that Mr. Wang is a good witness. "I think he is coming across as an honest person. There was no exaggerating. He didn't make up anything."

Leemie moves ahead to the technical parts of the prosecution, including the identification of the kidnappers in lineups. Then she asks, "And how did this ransom get paid?"

"My family in China contacted the person with the beeper number."

"Objection!" shouts the defense. Remember, the witness generally cannot repeat anything that he heard about from a third party. Lawyers have to be totally alert, ready to challenge any question, any phrase, or any single word by the opposing side.

"I'm going to stop the answer," the judge says. "Why don't we take a break, ladies and gentlemen, because this will take a few moments to resolve. We'll be with you in five or ten minutes, and then we'll work through to lunch."

The jury leaves the room.

The judge has anticipated the defense attorney's objection. "Is the objection on hearsay grounds?"

"Yes," agrees Glenn.

"Why isn't it classic hearsay?" Judge Fried asks the prosecutor. Remember, hearsay is repeating evidence you heard about from others.

Leemie is on the spot. "I don't know, judge, actually." A sheepish smile crosses her face.

The judge answers his own question. "It's classic hearsay. The objection is sustained. I will let you ask if he learned the ransom had been paid in China and end it at that. I don't see that as a problem."

Before they go back into session, Glenn has a few more requests on behalf of his client. He wants a better copy of the diagram of the apartment. He wants to know whether or not the detectives wrote memo entries about their conversations with this complaining witness. He wants any 911 tapes and any recordings made of telephone calls to Mr. Wang. Leemie doesn't think there are any, but she will check.

Once back in open court, the direct examination continues. Throughout this long morning, all members of the jury pay careful attention. No one fidgets, no one even yawns. Leemie asks, "Judge, may I proceed?"

"Yes."

"The woman who came with Johnny Ding, and who fed you the apple, was she there during the morning or nighttime?" she asks, setting the stage for a future witness.

"Night."

"I have no further questions." Leemie takes her seat.

CROSS-EXAMINATION

Glenn's job is to raise reasonable doubt about whether his client was actually one of the kidnappers. He will poke holes, show gaps, and expose any inconsistencies in Leemie's evidence.

"The standard practice in criminal defense is not only to show there is reasonable doubt, but also to give the jury an out," Glenn explains after the trial. "I was taught to give an alternative explanation consistent with the defendant's innocence."

Glenn walks toward the complaining witness with a friendly smile. The witness stiffens. "Mr. Wang, I represent Joe Chen, and I'm going to ask a number of questions now; okay?"

"Okay," Mr. Wang says, distrustful.

"If you don't understand the question, please let me know."

"What did you say?" he grunts.

"If you don't understand the question, please let me know, like you did right now."

"Okay."

"Did this happen about two and a half years ago?"

"This happened in 1995."

Glenn wants to show that this witness is unable to remember enough details to incriminate his client. "Is it fair to say your memory was better then than it is now?"

"Of course." Another grunt.

Glenn moves to a different line of questioning. "Do you recall telling Detective Hayman Goon that you were able to identify your kidnappers?"

"I did."

"Do you recall giving him the names of the kidnappers in this case?"

"I did."

"Do you recall telling him that there was an individual by the name of Johnny Ding who was involved in this kidnapping?"

The witness complains that the attorney is not pronouncing Chinese names correctly. "The name is Johnny *Ding*. Can you pronounce the name more correctly?"

"I don't mean to state anything incorrectly, Mr. Wang. And I assume that you will be better with Chinese names than I will be."

"Of course." The jury is smiling; some jurors smother laughter.

"We hope so," adds the judge. "Continue."

Mr. Wang is a sympathetic witness, and Glenn does not want to appear to be harassing him. "In the event that I mispronounce a name, please feel free to correct me."

"No problem," replies the witness, and grudgingly answers the question. "I did not say I was able to identify the leader. I said I was only able to identify some of the kidnappers."

Glenn tips his head sideways and asks if he once described Johnny Ding as being five feet nine inches tall. Leemie objects to this question, but Judge Fried allows it. Physical descriptions, especially height and weight, are a typical way to identify perpetrators. Mr. Wang does not remember saying that Johnny Ding is five feet nine inches tall.

As the defense attorney works, Leemie watches the jury's reactions and jots down questions she will use during the redirect examination. This comes after Glenn's cross. "I must be prepared to object if he's going for testimony that I don't think should come out."

While the cross-examination continues, Leemie is making a chart. On the left-hand side, she lists Glenn's main points. On the right-hand side, she writes questions to rebut his points. "Sometimes I'll even use different colored pens to clarify complex issues."

In rapid-fire sentences Glenn asks, "Do you recall telling the detective that Buddy Pan [Mr. Wang's friend from China] was one of those Asian males? Do you recall telling him that Buddy Pan had a gun? Do you recall telling Detective Goon that in September of 1995, Buddy Pan contacted you and threatened you about this kidnapping?"

"I did. I did. I did."

"Objection!" calls Leemie. She does not want Glenn badgering her witness.

The judge calms everyone down and calls for a lunch break. After the jury and the witness leave the courtroom, Judge Fried asks Leemie, "Objection to what?"

"Judge, he's trying to elicit something that Buddy Pan supposedly said to him which I think is hearsay."

Judge Fried replies, "I thought the question was whether he told the detective something Buddy Pan said to him."

Leemie knows where Glenn is going. "The next question will be, 'Didn't Buddy tell you...' That's when I objected."

Leemie is right. That is exactly where the defense attorney is going.

"What I'm trying to establish," Glenn explains to the judge, "is that there are other individuals involved in this kidnapping. On direct examination the witness claimed he did not know or could not identify all the perpetrators. But he later said he identified them in the beginning of the investigation. His current recollection is different from his original report. That's what I'm trying to establish." Glenn gallantly offers to withdraw or rephrase the question.

LUNCH BREAK

After lunch Glenn moves on to another topic. "Let's talk about an individual by the name of Buddy Pan. How do you know that person?"

"We were friends back in China."

"Did you have any arguments with him or fight with him on the boat ride over here?" Before the trial Glenn read about a disagreement in the detective's notes. Now he can use this information as a plausible motive for someone else's deciding to kidnap Mr. Wang.

"Had a fight with who?" It is not clear whether Mr. Wang does not understand or is just making life difficult for the defender.

"Buddy Pan."

"We had some disagreement," he admits reluctantly.

"On the boat?"

"Um-hmm."

"So you weren't friendly with him after the boat ride; is that correct?"

"We were still friends," the witness insists.

Glenn asks, "Now, Buddy Pan was one of the kidnappers; isn't that correct?"

"I cannot be definitely sure." Mr. Wang juts out his jaw contemptuously.

"Well, you told the police that he was one of the people who was involved in your kidnapping. Isn't that correct?"

"I didn't say that. I didn't say he was one of the kidnappers. No, I didn't."

"Is it your testimony that he did not have a gun during the kidnapping?"

"No, he didn't!" he shouts angrily.

"Noooooo?" The shock in Glenn's voice implies that this is not true. On to a new approach. "Now, Buddy Pan contacted you in September of 1995; is that correct?"

"After I was released from the kidnapping, he contacted me once. Exactly what was the date, I cannot remember."

Glenn nods as if to imply *There, there, you're doing fine.* Again Mr. Wang will not respond. "When he contacted you, he threatened you not to report this kidnapping to the police. Is that correct?"

"He said this: 'Whatever the loss you suffer, that's already—it's over. If you report to the police, it's not going to make much difference.' That's what he said."

"Isn't it true that Buddy Pan is involved in a gang that commits crimes in the Baltimore area?"

"Objection!" says Leemie.

"Let's go to the side, please," the judge says.

Once aside, Leemie objects because this information is not relevant to the kidnapping; she maintains it has nothing to do with it. The judge asks Glenn how this issue is relevant. He replies that Johnny Ding, who is one of the future cooperating witnesses, committed crimes in the Baltimore area. Johnny Ding and Buddy Pan are somehow connected.

The judge doesn't see this point as relevant. He sustains the objection.

"What grounds?" Glenn demands.

"Completely irrelevant," Judge Fried snaps back. "Those are the grounds." Back to open court.

Glenn must establish the fact that Johnny Ding is one very bad man. And he must establish that this very bad man is the leader of the kidnappers. He asks Mr. Wang if Johnny Ding ever pointed a gun to his head. Did he hit him? How often did he beat the other victim? Did he order Sonny Chen to beat him?

Mr. Wang says, "I was always blindfolded during the period of time. I was hit by a lot of people. I do not know who hit me."

"Is it fair to say that people were coming in and out of the apartment and spoke to the kidnappers, but did not harm you?"

"I was hit by a lot of people," he repeats.

Glenn switches back to the time Mr. Wang first arrived in America. He asks what it was like to be held in captivity by the brutal snake heads. Mr. Wang says, "If you don't have money to pay them, they will hit you really, really hard. If, coincidentally, they hit you to death, that's what you get."

As Glenn continues to ask questions about Sonny Chen and the snake heads, Leemie objects to every one. They are not relevant to this kidnapping. Although every objection is sustained, Glenn doesn't seem to mind. He is planting seeds of doubt for future witnesses. Besides, the members of the jury hear the questions, even though legally they must pretend they did not.

"I have no further questions."

Mr. Wang breathes a deep sigh.

REDIRECT AND RECROSS

During her direct examination of a witness, Leemie lets the witness tell the story in a free-flowing way. With redirect she zeros in to clarify issues that Glenn brought up during his cross. How did Jane Ding get his phone number? (From Buddy Pan.) Did he ever actually see Buddy Pan in the apartment? (No.) Did the kidnapping leave him emotional and fearful? (Yes.) Does he believe that Johnny Ding and Charlie Chan are two different persons? (Yes. They are different.)

Once she has no further questions, the defense has a chance to recross. The rules for recross are the same as redirect. Glenn can ask questions that relate to Leemie's redirect only. In this way the testimony gets narrower and narrower, like water pouring down a funnel.

Glenn stands by his client at the defense table as a subtle way to remind the jurors that this witness cannot identify his client. He says, "This individual you referred to as Johnny Ding, was he the person with the sunglasses?"

"That's right."

"And that person made phone calls to China. Correct?"

"He did."

"As a matter of fact, he was the individual who forced you on numerous occasions to speak to your family in China. Correct?"

"He did force me to talk to my family, but not a number of times."

There are no further questions.

The judge calls for a short break before the next witness, the second kidnapping victim, Mr. Li, is called.

Both Leemie and Glenn are pleased with their examinations. Leemie was able to humanize the crime because Mr. Wang was a very believable witness. Glenn was able to raise some reasonable doubt that his client was a kidnapper because Mr. Wang was unable to positively identify him. So far so good.

# DAILO

- LEEMIE HAS THE SECOND COMPLAINING WITNESS TAKE THE STAND.
- MR. LI TELLS THE COURT ABOUT HIS KIDNAPPING.
- GLENN TRIES TO GET HIM TO ADMIT THAT HE CANNOT IDENTIFY JOE CHEN.

"The People call Mr. Li."

I took a bus to New York on August 3, at seven or eight in the morning. I came for an immigration hearing in court the following day. At that time I had a friend who I was to meet at a restaurant here in Chinatown.

At the bus station I ran into Charlie Chan [the real Johnny Ding]. We talked a little bit. He asked me why I was going to New York. I told him I had to go to court. Then I told him I did not know anything about New York and I have to meet a friend at a restaurant. He said, "I am very familiar with New York. I'll show you around." We rode in the same bus to New York City. When we arrived at 42nd Street, he made a phone call. I waited for him outside. There were so many people, so much noise, it was impossible for me to hear what he said.

Then he called a taxi and he said, "I will ride in the cab with you."

He told me he will take me to the place I have to go, but first he wanted to drop off his bag in his apartment. Then, after the cab ride, he made another phone call.

I remember we were standing by a subway station, and after a while, somebody else walked out from the station. This other person walked with us to the apartment.

When we arrived in front of his apartment, Charlie said he didn't have the key. He had to call somebody to come out and open the door for him.

Unlike Mr. Wang, Mr. Li did not want to testify in court about his kidnapping. He would have preferred to have the ordeal simply go away. But Mr. Wang convinced the twenty-two-year-old to come forward. "We're doing this for the good of other people," Mr. Wang told him, "so this won't happen again."

Mr. Li was so frightened that he would not travel to New York alone. Detective David Chan, a member of the New York City Major Case Squad, told me that "the victims had to come in a number of times, for hearings or lineups. We had to go to Baltimore to get Li. One time he wasn't even home. He went to work. The Baltimore detectives and we had to do a whole, separate investigation just to find out where he worked. We spent two days hunting him out. He was totally shocked that we found him."

· · ·

Mr. Li has the romantic features of a Chinese Leonardo DiCaprio: high cheekbones and deep, sulky eyes. For the last three years he has worked in a Chinese restaurant in Baltimore. The hours are long, from nine-thirty in the morning to nine-thirty at night, six days a week. He works to repay his family the original $33,000 fee they paid a snake head to smuggle him to America, plus the additional $8,000 they paid the kidnappers for his release.

.   .   .

Back in the courtroom it is four o'clock and Mr. Li looks exhausted. It is a good time to break for the day. Judge Fried dismisses the jury but the lawyers and the judge remain. There are other legal issues to resolve. First, the telephone records are still under protective order, and Glenn still wants them released. Leemie vigorously objects. "These are the telephone numbers of my victims in China. Joe Chen would not necessarily remember those numbers. I don't want him to have access to these documents before necessary. I need to protect the victims' families."

The prosecutor knows that eventually she has to reveal this evidence to the defense. She is willing to release the phone records so long as they are limited to Glenn's eyes only. "Just me, Glenn Garber," the defense attorney agrees, looking up at the judge.

Glenn then reminds the judge that he also still wants the records that involve the case of his client's brother, Sonny Chen. Although the judge originally said he would wait until the brother is called as a witness, he changes his mind and tells Leemie to have them available tomorrow morning.

Court is adjourned. The lawyers return to their offices and continue working on their strategies.

TIME: FRIDAY, APRIL 17, 1998; 10:00 A.M.
PLACE: NEW YORK STATE SUPREME COURTHOUSE

Outside the courtroom jurors sip coffee, read the morning newspaper, and wait. Inside the courtroom Joe Chen sits passively at the defense table while Glenn approaches the bench. He asks for a separation order. Glenn does not want the witnesses, especially witnesses who have already confessed to the crime, anywhere near his client. Because Glenn may call some of them to testify, he doesn't want Leemie to try to argue that they changed their stories to help Joe.

Judge Fried agrees, saying he will call prison officials next.

Glenn just received the material he asked for yesterday. He asks for a brief recess after the direct examination for time to review the material. The judge agrees again and tells the guard to bring in the jurors.

Once the jurors are seated, Leemie asks Mr. Li what happened after he arrived at the apartment.

Charlie Chan made a call from outside. Someone from the apartment below came up and opened the door. Charlie Chan said, "Come in. Come in and hang out for a little while. As soon as I put my bag down, I will take you out."

When I entered I saw people in the kitchen. I walked further in. Charlie Chan kept saying, "Come in. Come in. Sit down."

When I entered, I was kidnapped. Luke Chen [Cow Eyes] had a gun and started hitting me with it, saying, "Do you know what is happening to you?"

Sonny Chen was also hitting me. At first I fought back because I knew what was happening to me. It lasted about ten minutes. Charlie Chan went into a different room.

After the beating I was blindfolded with a sky-blue T-shirt. My hands were bound. Another person came in and asked me for my telephone number in China.

There was a girl in the kitchen. Then another person came in, but I was already blindfolded and could not see his face.

As soon as that person walked in, he demanded my number and I was told to speak to my family. Each time I was on the phone, I was beaten.

*Originally they demanded 280,000 yuan [approximately $34,000].
Later it was negotiated down to 200,000 [$24,000]. The final amount
was $8,000 U.S.*

*While I was being beaten, they threatened me. A knife was brought out
and Cow Eyes said, "I'm going to cut off your finger." And he also said,
"You know, there are many people who die in New York and they never
find the cause."*

While questioning Mr. Li, Leemie stands at an angle so the jury can
easily see both of them. Some jurors lean over to see if Mr. Li is missing a finger. He is not.

Leemie walks to the center of the well of the courtroom, pauses dramatically, and asks about the unidentified man who demanded his telephone number in China. "Did you ever hear that person being referred
to by name or nickname?"

"Others called him *dailo*."

THE DAILO

"In the underground society," Mr. Li explains, "dailo is considered
the top guy."

Leemie asks, "Was Charlie Chan ever referred to as the dailo during
the time that you were there?"

"Not during the time I was there. No. I didn't hear that. As far as I
knew there was Charlie Chan, Cow Eyes, Sonny Chen, and the dailo."

Glenn is listening to the testimony, thinking, "This is bad for my
client." After the trial, Glenn says that nothing showed up in the
reports about a dailo, a big boss. "The detectives took pretty decent
notes. Now, all of a sudden, this dailo concept surfaces in a fairly powerful way. I believe it was manufactured by the prosecution."

.　.　.

Leemie focuses on the beatings. The victims were brutally beaten for the slightest infractions. For example, someone, we are not yet told who, saw Mr. Li move his hand to a more comfortable position. When the dailo was told about it, he ordered Sonny Chen to hit him.

.　.　.

Leemie then turns her line of questioning to another incident that will come up again and again throughout the trial.

> *Charlie Chan's girlfriend came to the apartment. She asked if I owed a smuggling debt, and if I did, I should pay it soon and be released. She thought I was there because I owed money to the snake head for my smuggler's fee to America.*
>
> *I told her this has nothing to do with that. Charlie Chan brought me here.*
>
> *The next day Charlie Chan hit me. He said, "How could you tell my girlfriend about this? How could you tell her that I was the one who brought you here?"*
>
> *There was another man with him. I didn't see him, I only heard his voice. This fifth man was different from the dailo.*
>
> *Before they released me, my family called the kidnappers. My father demanded to hear my voice. I spoke to my father over the phone.*

"You got a phone call from your father?" the judge interrupts.

"Yes."

"Objection!" calls Glenn, predicting that the next question will be hearsay.

"Sustained!" replies the judge, overruling the anticipated line of questioning. The witness cannot repeat conversations that he did not take part in or overhear personally. It is considered hearsay if Mr. Li reports a conversation his father claimed he had with a third person. Lawyers and judges seem to have an uncanny intuition about approaching hearsay testimony.

Leemie asks the witness how often the dailo visited the apartment.

"I do not know," he replies, "but when he came the first time, he took the telephone number."

Mr. Li can describe the dailo's girlfriend. "She was a little taller than the other women and had long legs and long hair. I remember one time when she came in, she had a skirt on." Li was able to see her legs and lower torso because the tape left a little room exposed on the two sides of his nose. But he was unable to see her face. But he saw her hair. "The dailo's girlfriend's hair was long." A juror looks at Joe Chen for a sign, a signal, any sense of recognition. Nothing. Joe does not react one way or the other about the dailo or a girlfriend with long hair. It is as if he is in another place, far, far away from these proceedings.

Leemie asks, "Mr. Li, did she ask you anything about how you got to the apartment?"

"Objection."

"Sustained."

Leemie rephrases the questions. "Mr. Li, what else, if anything, did she say to you?"

"Objection," says Glenn.

"Objection overruled."

Later Glenn explains, "During direct, we are supposed to ask open-ended questions because we are trying to draw the story from the witness: 'What happened next? What happened after that?' You would never ask, for example, 'Did Joe Chen pick up

> **JUDGE FRIED SAYS:**
> In most instances a lawyer cannot lead the witness during direct examination. For example, the phrase "What did she say?" assumes that something was said and is, therefore, leading the witness.
>
> A good lawyer can easily convert a leading question to a non-leading question by adding two words, "if anything."
>
> "What, if anything, did she say?" does not assume something was said, and that makes the question not leading.

the telephone when the call came to the house?' You would ask, 'What happened during this time period when the call came?'

"Cross-examination is different. The skill in a cross-examination is to ask questions that keep control of the answers, close-ended questions. The lawyer will ask, 'Isn't it true that after you took a plea, you met with the investigators?' The answer can only be 'yes,' 'no,' or 'I don't remember.' " During the cross, because the witness is considered hostile, lawyers are allowed to ask leading questions. The lawyer wants to avoid unasked-for explanations that could hurt his or her case. Actually, with permission from the judge, lawyers are usually allowed to ask leading, close-ended questions with all hostile witnesses—even during direct examination. This happens later when Glenn presents his defense.

> **HOSTILE WITNESS:**
> If a witness exhibits animosity or partiality under direct examination, the lawyer is allowed to cross-examine him, that is, treat him as though he had been called by the opposite party.

. . .

Judge Fried stops the proceedings to give the jury a break and tells the defense attorney that he will now have twenty minutes to talk with his client. Then, after the direct, he will give him an additional ten minutes. "It takes ten minutes just to go down and up the steps to the holding cell," Glenn complains, stops himself, and adds, "Your Honor."

The defense attorney must have ample time to talk with his client. "Let's see what happens. You can go down with your client now. We'll bring you back at a quarter after."

Twenty minutes later Glenn returns, very, very upset. Although Joe Chen is in a separate holding pen on one floor, the other witnesses, those who have already confessed to the kidnapping, are all together on another floor. He wants everyone separated. He doesn't want the potential witnesses to have time together to come up with a new story.

Judge Fried issues an order that everybody be separated even though he knows it is a logistical nightmare for the guards and detectives. Glenn thanks the judge and says, "I need the opportunity to state things on the record. [If Joe Chen is found guilty, he will use this record to appeal his conviction to the higher courts.] I apologize for being a stumbling block, but this is important."

> **APPEAL:**
> To ask a superior court to review the decision of a lower court.

"You do not need to apologize for anything," Judge Fried says. The defense attorney must use any and all legal avenues to ensure that his client has a fair trial.

The jury returns. The judge believes an explanation to the jury is in order. "These delays probably seem crazy to you, but this case is unusual," he tells them. "Because we are dealing with a language barrier and a number of witnesses, this takes an extra amount of time, especially since we need interpreters. I want you to know we haven't been twiddling our thumbs." Many in the jury nod and smile at the judge.

Once Mr. Li is back on the stand, Glenn objects to every one of Leemie's questions as leading. He is always overruled. The judge has the discretion to allow leading questions during a direct examination not only when the witness is hostile, but also when, for example, there is a language barrier or a cultural obstruction, or if the witness is a child or elderly. A certain amount of leading might be necessary to clarify the testimony.

Finally, out of exasperation, Glenn asks to approach the bench. "I would like the record to reflect a standing objection to all leading questions," he says.

Judge Fried easily agrees to the standing objection, and they go back to open court and work till lunch.

．　．　．

"All right, counsels, back to the phone records." Judge Fried asks Leemie after lunch, while the jurors wait outside the courtroom, "How can Mr. Garber be denied permission to consult with his client with regard to those particular phone numbers? They are evidence in this case."

Leemie knows she has to turn over all her evidence. But her night in the law library studying case law paid off. "They are not in evidence at this time," she replies. "Until the investigator from Bell Atlantic puts them into evidence, I would feel more comfortable *not* having those records shown to the defendant." On the surface Glenn is polite and professional. Inside he is fuming.

Part of the defense is based on the fact that the phone records show that Joe moved out of the apartment long before the kidnapping took place. If Joe Chen chooses to testify on his own behalf, this will definitely come up.

But Leemie is unyielding. "A protective order shall stay in effect. Joe Chen must not see the telephone numbers." She repeats, "I want to protect the victim's families."

Glenn is angry, no question about it. Here is an example from his point of view of when the law is not entirely fair. Glenn explains later, "Technically, she does not have to hand the stuff over to me until the witness testifies. To her credit, she is applying disclosure procedures to her advantage. But Judge Fried said that the materials should be turned over to me well in advance; otherwise it could hamper my ability to effectively represent my client. There is no great case law on this for me. There are constitutional principles to rely upon—the client's right to a fair trial—but to my knowledge there is no rule in New York State saying that she has to disclose witness statements ahead of time. Names of witnesses, yes, their testimony, no. So I am stuck. She knows that there is a lot of material I have to review when she gives it to me, and she is playing the rules to her advantage by holding it until the last minute. It pretty much puts me at an informational disadvantage."

Another obstacle for Glenn: The prosecutor's second cooperating witness, Johnny Ding, is in federal custody for a different crime, a murder. Leemie has talked to the assistant United States attorney who is in charge of that case. He told her that on one occasion he wrote about a page of notes. Leemie has requested the notes, but the U.S. attorney refuses to turn them over. She tells the judge, "Unless Your Honor is going to order him to turn over these notes, he said he would not."

The judge is willing to sign the order.

"If necessary," Leemie replies, and looks over at Glenn. He could save her an awful lot of time and trouble if he would work without the notes. Glenn remains silent; this is her problem. Finally Glenn adds his two cents. "I obviously want the notes."

Leemie raises her voice. "The assistant attorney is the chief of the Violent Gang Unit in the Eastern District!" She turns to the judge and lowers her voice respectfully. "Sometimes it's difficult for me to reach him over lunch hour. Can I have a little leeway this afternoon?"

"Certainly," the judge replies. The judge likes it when everyone is civil to one another.

AFTERNOON SESSION—CROSS-EXAMINATION

Glenn approaches Mr. Li, who is still under oath. "Good afternoon, Mr. Li. I am going to ask you a few questions about the perpetrator you referred to as Charlie Chan." The witness does not look at the defense attorney. Glenn tries to draw out an accurate description of Johnny Ding, better known to this witness as Charlie Chan. As Mr. Li struggles to do this, Glenn asks, "Things have gotten less certain to you, is that correct?"

"Objection."

"Calls for a 'yes' or 'no,'" says the judge. "Answer the question."

Mr. Li looks at Glenn. "Yes. To me, I know that my memory of it is not as good about it as it was in the past, but these things happened to me, an experience I will always remember."

Leemie reaches for her legal pad and writes the phrase "*these things happened to me, an experience I will always remember,*" and files it in a folder marked SUMMATION. Later, when she prepares her closing address to the jury, she will think of ways to dramatically use this line.

Glenn knows that the witness was allowed to say too much. He tells himself to keep it simple. "I'm not questioning whether or not this happened. Nor am I questioning whether or not this was a terrible incident or time in your life. I'm just questioning you about details, how the ability to recall details becomes more difficult as time passes."

The witness nods curtly and his shoulders rise.

"Isn't it true, Mr. Li, that you told the detectives that Charlie Chan was six feet tall?"

"I did not say that to them. No. I did not say that to them." But Glenn has a report that he did say that to the police.

"I have no further questions."

Leemie jumps from her seat for redirect. When Mr. Li was first questioned by the local police in his town, some of the substance in their report was not accurate. Leemie later explains, "I wanted it clear that our Major Case Squad detectives did not make the errors. Otherwise their credibility could come into question later, when they are on the stand. This may be a small detail, but it's these small details that actually make a difference in a trial."

"I have just one or two questions. Mr. Li, when you first reported this to the police, was it to the police in your hometown?"

"I reported it to the police in my hometown."

"And at that time did you meet Detectives Chan or Goon?"

"No."

"No further questions." And she quickly returns to her seat.

Now it's Glenn's turn again. He throws questions at the witness. What did he tell the police? What did he tell the detectives? How did he describe his captors? The lawyer and witness go round and round and round. Height... weight... height. Glenn pushes for the minutest of details. The jury fidgets. Glenn sees them. He can't risk losing the jury. "No further questions," he says abruptly, and the witness is excused.

Mr. Li practically dives out of the witness box and quickly leaves by the back door. The jury is asked to leave the courtroom for just a few minutes.

Glenn is not happy with this cross-examination. Somehow he must find a clearer way to emphasize to the jurors the significance of the inaccuracy of the testimony about the kidnappers' heights. Both complaining witnesses said that the leader, the dailo, is the tallest kidnapper. In fact, the tallest kidnapper is Cow Eyes, who is five foot eleven. All the other men, including Joe Chen, are about five five.

Glenn asks the judge for a continuance. He says that he has not had enough time to interview the upcoming witnesses and talk with his client because the interpreters were not available.

> **CONTINUANCE:**
> This is the adjournment or postponement of a trial.

Judge Fried offers to stop the trial for one full day. He'll arrange for Joe Chen and the other imprisoned witnesses to be brought to the courthouse where Glenn can interview them. "I'll produce everybody in this building on Monday. I'll bring your client into the courtroom at two-thirty and I'll ask Ms. Kahng to be here as well. We'll settle whatever issues need to be resolved. I will tell the jurors we're not in session Monday."

"There are still some other matters I need to discuss," Glenn says.

Judge Fried leans back in his chair. "I'm here the rest of the day."

.   .   .

After talking with his lawyer, Joe Chen is handcuffed and taken back to his cell. Glenn then returns to his office. He has an appointment with Suzy Ling, his client's girlfriend. There are many questions he must ask her in order to prepare her as a witness for the defense.

He waits for her. And he waits. And he waits. Finally Glenn calls his wife for the second day in a row. "Don't hold dinner, I'm running late."

He waits.

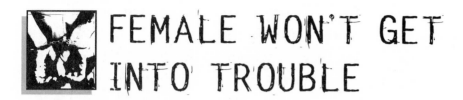# FEMALE WON'T GET INTO TROUBLE

- COOPERATING WITNESS 1: JANE DING.
- LEEMIE QUESTIONS JANE DING ABOUT HER TRIP TO AMERICA, AND THE
  WITNESS FILLS IN DETAILS ABOUT THE KIDNAPPING.

TIME: TUESDAY, APRIL 21, 1998; 9:45 A.M.
PLACE: JUDGE FRIED'S COURTROOM

The Statue of Liberty and the American flag. That's the design on the wide bold tie Joe Chen wears to court on this day. Yesterday, after court, Glenn urged his client to connect with the jury. "Show more emotion. You have to get the jury to care about you," Glenn said. Perhaps this patriotic tie is Joe Chen's way to win the hearts of the jury. Judge Fried observes the fashion statement, but shows no noticeable reaction. Instead he directs his attention to the lawyers. "Is there anything we need to do before the jurors are brought in?"

Glenn fiddles with his legal pad. He is very, very angry. After his talk with Joe, he returned to his office for a meeting with his client's girlfriend. She never showed up. "She was picked up by the police," says

Glenn. He is certain that she was interrogated about her potential testimony in this case.

It is the defense lawyer's job to prod and probe anything and everything that could hurt the defendant. He can't let his guard down. He can't assume that anything could happen by chance. Glenn tries to control his indignation, but sarcasm seeps through his voice when complaining about the state's action. "I'm asking for an inquiry by the court to find out the circumstances of this because—I'm not alleging this has risen to the level of witness tampering—the circumstances do raise some concern." Witness tampering is a serious offense and could result in a mistrial.

Leemie Kahng is usually very calm. This is not one of those times. "She was *not* arrested," Leemie insists. "I told Mr. Garber that she was not arrested. She was a witness to a robbery."

"What do you want me to do, Mr. Garber?" asks the judge, massaging his forehead.

"I want this on record, just in case there is a problem later on."

"Next!" says Judge Fried.

. . .

JUDGE FRIED SAYS:
The state has more resources, money, and power than a single individual. To level the playing field between the prosecutor (the state) and the individual (the defendant), rules have been set up to benefit the defendant.

As examples, a prosecutor cannot spring evidence on the defense. The defendant has the right to know about the prosecutor's witnesses—including what is known as "prior bad acts"—before the witness's testimony.

Another challenge. As far as Glenn is concerned, he has not been given evidence in a timely manner. Just this morning he learned about two "prior bad acts" committed by the next witness, the informant Jane Ding.

Jane Ding is one of the convicted kidnappers. During Glenn's cross-examination of her, he will try to convince the jury that she is not trustworthy, that she will say absolutely anything to get a lighter jail sentence. One way to do this is to show that Jane has been involved in other crimes. (The rules regarding the admissibility of the "prior bad acts" of the defendant are different. That will come up later in the trial.)

Leemie says that she does not have copies of those arrests because they are sealed, closed against inspection. Leemie guesses that Jane probably received a disorderly conduct violation, which is cleared from her record after a year. Since that is not a criminal conviction, sealing the arrests protects her privacy.

Judge Fried offers to sign a subpoena to unseal the documents.

Next!

The defense attorney wants more information about another future cooperating witness, Johnny Ding. Remember, Johnny Ding is a snake head who was involved in smuggling Sonny Chen, Jane Ding, and the first victim, Mr. Wang, to America. He is also part of the kidnapping team; he brought the second victim to the apartment. In addition, he is the witness who pleaded guilty to a murder. Glenn refers to Johnny Ding as "one bad dude."

When Johnny Ding committed the murder, he wasn't alone. His partner was a gang leader, a dailo. Glenn wants the name of that leader, to show the jury that there are any number of people who are called dailo. But a United States attorney does not want the name revealed because it could affect an ongoing investigation.

> **JUDGE FRIED SAYS:**
> The U.S. attorney is part of the federal court system. Federal law—the law of the United States—generally overrides state law.

The judge tells Glenn, "I'm not going to allow you to ask that witness whether he was charged with somebody who is described in the indictment as dailo because it may all be irrelevant. If a federal indictment is sealed, I don't have the power to unseal it."

Glenn's mouth drops in disbelief. Judge Fried sees the look on the defense's face. "It's completely irrelevant." The judge looks down at the defense attorney. "That may seem to you—with the look on your face—as a ruling that I should not make, but that's my ruling." Pause. "You can ask him whether he was indicted with someone else."

"The reason I have that expression on my face," replies Glenn, "is that I think it's a little bit premature to make a ruling without hearing what the witness has to say."

"If the witness's own testimony opens it up, that's different," the judge rules.

With a wave of his hand, Judge Fried says, "Bring in the jurors."

The jurors enter the courtroom, drop their coats and bags on the front two rows for spectators, and take their appointed seats in the jury box. "Good morning, ladies and gentlemen. We are ready to proceed." The judge asks the prosecutor to call her next witness.

"The People call Jane Ding."

Jane Ding enters the courtroom and glances over to where Joe Chen is seated. He does not acknowledge his former family member at all.

Jane is a slim twenty-one-year-old of average height. Her face, though pleasant, is unremarkable. She has a blunt-cut hair style that just about reaches her shoulders. A dash of lipstick highlights full, rounded lips. Jane is dressed for court in a casual black pants suit and a white T-shirt with tiny blue embroidered flowers.

Mary Cassidy administers the oath, and Jane answers, "Uh-huh."

Mary asks, "Yes?"

> **THE OATH:**
> "Do you solemnly swear that the evidence that you shall give this Court and to this Jury in the action of the People of the State of New York versus Joe Chen shall be the truth, the whole truth, and nothing but the truth, so help you God?"

"Yes," says Jane, her voice barely audible.

Leemie questions the witness.

I came on a boat. In China, I was married to the cousin of Joe Chen—he's over there with the glasses on. I have a child, a boy. He is still in China. He is five. My husband is still in China.

When we were in China, my husband wanted to come to the United States. My parents paid the snake head $20,000 U.S. to put him on a boat. But before he left China, Chinese policemen came and arrested everyone on the boat. He went to prison for one year. When he returned home, he wanted to try again.

After he left a second time, I cried a lot. Later on I placed my son at my mom's home and got on another boat to follow him here. I was on the boat three months. I arrived, he did not. His boat was returned to China.

After I arrived in the United States, a snake head said I have to pay $27,000. We were held at a house until our families paid the money. The snake head wanted the females to sleep with him. If you don't do it, he would hit you.

Later I was released. Another snake head drove me to Chinatown. My aunt's husband met me and took me to a massage place that his family owned. [In this particular situation, "massage place" implies "a house of prostitution."] I was so scared. I called Johnny Ding's pager. We were from the same village in China. We were neighbors.

Johnny Ding came and took me to a house in Brooklyn. I stayed there for two days, but the house was owned by someone else, and they didn't want me to stay there.

I walked the streets. It was raining heavily. Johnny Ding called his girlfriend. She gave me some clothes. I stayed there for two or three days. Later on, she got me work in a garment factory. In my next apartment I shared a bed with two other women. I went to work at seven A.M. and came home at midnight.

I was interested in working in a restaurant because my parents had a restaurant back in China. I have a relative who owns a restaurant in Montana. I moved there to Montana and worked in the restaurant for four months—from ten A.M. to ten-thirty P.M., six days a week. Every month I sent a payment back to China.

A friend told me I could get a C-8 card—that is a legal status to use for a working permit. I returned to New York and went to the immigration center for an interview for it. I saw Sonny Chen, who was there for an interview too. He gave me his beeper number. I called him quite often. I think that was in '95.

I went back to work in Montana, but I was so lonely over there. All the people I knew were here, in Chinatown.

I returned to New York about June 1995. I paged Sonny and he took me to his place. Joe Chen and his girlfriend were there. Luke Chen was there. His nickname is Lew Mook, Cow Eyes.

I lived in the apartment. I didn't find a job yet. No one was working but Joe Chen's girlfriend. She used to work at a restaurant, and then a massage place.

Leemie has called Jane Ding as a witness because she has inside information that the two blindfolded victims could not give. She was also present for the planning of the first kidnapping. After the trial, Leemie explained, "I thought it was instrumental to develop how the kidnapping came about and what they planned. The planning was important because according to Jane, the defendant directed them to do certain things. This goes to the theory that Joe Chen was the leader, the dailo. She is the only one who could provide that information. Even Johnny Ding [the next witness] couldn't provide that information. He wasn't part of the original planning; he came along with the second victim."

Prompted by more questions, Jane describes the planning and execution of the kidnapping. She explains that at first Joe didn't say much. He only said, "Female won't get into any trouble. You ask him to come out and bring him over to this house and then you won't have any involvement for the rest of the incident."

The prosecutor asks why Mr. Wang was selected.

"Because he came here on the same boat as I came here. And the first reason was that they knew his relatives was in—"

"Objection!" Glenn calls, picking up on the word "knew."

As he did with the two earlier witnesses, Judge Fried explains hearsay. "You can't tell what they *knew*, only what they *said*."

"They said . . . they knew that this person was in restaurant business."

"Objection!"

The judge is patient with the witness. "Is that what they *said*? You can only tell us what somebody said."

Leemie tries to clean up the testimony by rephrasing the question. "You heard that Mr. Wang's family was in the restaurant business?"

"Yes, because we talked about it on the boat." Jane heaves a sigh. "I don't know exactly why we chose him." As the witness continues, Glenn jots down notes on a legal pad, statements he will use later in his cross-examination.

Jane continues, "We talked about if Mr. Wang asks why we do this, we just tell him because you came from Johnny Ding's boat. You didn't pay money to Johnny Ding. That was the excuse we are going to use to ask his family member to pay the money."

"Whose idea was it to use Johnny Ding's name?"

"Joe Chen," she says, not daring to look over at the defendant.

They move on to how Jane lured the first victim to their apartment.

"I and Cow Eyes went to Chinatown at the subway station. I didn't know my way. Me and Mr. Wang walked together. Cow Eyes led the way but did not make his presence known. Mr. Wang said he was hungry, so we went to a snack place. He had a bowl of *gorbien*."

"Can you describe what kind of food it is?" the prosecutor asks.

Jane misunderstands. "You use the rice and you mix up in the blender and then you turn on the stove. Okay. You mix with water, and you turn on the stove, and you just pull it around the wok. Okay. Then you put in soup, and then you put in some vegetables, some meat, slice meat..."

Oblivious to the jury's snickers, Jane goes on and on. Leemie allows her to ramble. It can do no harm. Besides, it further points out how very unsophisticated this witness is.

"After he ate, we went to the apartment," Jane finally says. "Cow Eyes was waiting outside. I opened the door with a key. I went to the bedroom."

"Where was Joe Chen?"

"Objection!" calls Glenn.

The judge corrects the line of questioning, "Was Joe Chen in the apartment when you entered?"

"Sonny, Cow Eyes, and Joe were in the apartment. Joe was in the room located in the back. He was not in this room."

"Was anyone wearing sunglasses?"

"Cow Eyes." Some jurors lean forward. Glenn jots down that answer. This helps his case because the second victim testified that the dailo was the only person who wore sunglasses.

Jane explains that Joe opened the back bedroom door for her. "He asked, 'Are you afraid?' I said, 'A little bit.' I don't remember anything else. I only remember this phrase."

AFTERNOON SESSION

After the lunch break, Leemie continues her direct examination. "Earlier this morning you were describing some things that happened in the apartment when Mr. Wang was first brought in. Was Johnny Ding involved in Mr. Wang's kidnapping?"

"No."

Leemie moves on to the second victim. Jane describes the time she saw the second victim, Mr. Li. "He was brought to the bedroom in the back. His hands were tied up and his eyes were blindfolded with clothes. Johnny Ding hit him and said, 'If your family don't give us the money, I will put you in a bag and throw you in the ocean.' "

．　　．　　．

Stroke by stroke, like painting a picture, the prosecutor uses Jane Ding's testimony to fill in the facts of her case. Leemie's next stroke is meant to support her theory that Joe Chen is the dailo, the leader of the kidnappers.

Jane says, "Joe Chen was the oldest and he has been in the United States the longest time. In Chinese culture the oldest is the more mature. The oldest brother or sister in the family has to take care of the younger sister or brother. Whatever Joe Chen said, Sonny Chen would listen. Cow Eyes, too, because he was younger; that's part of the reason."

The Chen family was soon enmeshed in another complication. This one was between Jane and Sonny. Leemie asks about it before Glenn can use it in his defense. Jane says, "I and Sonny were good friends. I always talked to him and trusted him. I didn't have many relatives or friends. Only Sonny Chen I was able to talk to. He was very good. We became boyfriend and girlfriend. I loved him."

Soon after their romance blossomed, Jane Ding began working as a prostitute in her uncle's massage parlor. She describes her life as a prostitute, the raids, the many arrests. Tears trickle down her cheeks. A guard brings her the box of tissues from Mary Cassidy's desk.

Leemie interrupts her own questioning to ask for a sidebar. A reporter from a local Chinese newspaper is taking notes in the otherwise empty gallery. Leemie is worried about what could happen if Jane's name is mentioned in the press. Other gang members will know that she is informing on Joe. Snitches have a way of getting hurt.

Leemie also wants to protect the names of the two victims and their families back in China.

But a trial is a public forum, and a judge does not have the legal authority to keep the press out of the courtroom. Nothing can be done.

．　．　．

> **COOPERATION AGREEMENT:**
> This is a written understanding between a prosecutor and a defendant and his or her lawyer. Generally the defendant agrees to plead guilty and to give information and/or testify. In exchange, the prosecutor will give a recommendation to the sentencing judge. It is only a recommendation; the sentencing judge has the final say.

Two years ago Jane was arrested for this kidnapping and has remained in jail ever since. When she pleaded guilty, she was facing a minimum sentence of six to eighteen years and a maximum sentence of eight and a half to twenty-five years. Sonny Chen and Cow Eyes faced the same sentence.

Then Jane learned that she could be given a lower sentence if she cooperates with the authorities and tells them who else was involved. In separate meetings, with their lawyers present, the two men were given the same opportunity.

Leemie asks, "Did there come a time when you entered into an agreement with my office?"

"Yes."

"Is this agreement still in effect?"

"Yes."

"What is your understanding of it?"

"I have to tell the whole thing of this incident. If I lie, I will receive six to eighteen years. If I tell the truth, it will be reduced to three to nine years."

"As part of this agreement, did you give information about Johnny Ding's involvement?"

"Yes."

There are no further questions and the jury is excused for the day.

TIME: WEDNESDAY, APRIL 22, 1998; 9:30 A.M.
PLACE: OUTSIDE JUDGE FRIED'S COURTROOM

Jane Ding is missing.

NOW I DON'T TRUST NOBODY

- GLENN CROSS-EXAMINES JANE DING.
- JANE DING AVOIDS HIS QUESTIONS.
- LEEMIE TRIES TO PROTECT HER WITNESS.

TIME: WEDNESDAY, APRIL 22, 1998; 10:30 A.M.
PLACE: INSIDE THE COURTROOM

Detective David Chan rushes into the courtroom. "There is one more bus arriving from Riker's Island [the prison] at eleven o'clock. She may be on that bus!"

"Let me tell you what happened," Judge Fried, rubbing his forehead, says to the jury. "It's no wonder I haven't any hair left." They smile at him as he shrugs his shoulders. "As you know, the witness who was supposed to be here this morning is in jail. She must be transported to this building by law enforcement personnel.

"There's been a glitch. We don't know what the glitch is yet, and we can't find out whether she has, in fact, left. I know it's going to take at least half an hour. If she is not on that bus, it might take all morning.

"Normally there would be other witnesses available to squeeze in, but we fully expected that she would be on the stand all morning, and I authorized the assistant district attorney not to have any additional witnesses ready." He smiles at Leemie. "She can blame me for it. So have a pleasant walk outside, if that's what you would like to do. You can remain in the hallway. I'm going to use this time in the courtroom to take care of some business that I need to with the lawyers. I ask for your understanding. Come back at eleven o'clock. Sorry for this delay."

Just after the last juror leaves the courtroom, the telephone rings. It's the prison. Jane Ding is on a special bus that will bring her to this building. If the traffic holds, she should be here by eleven-thirty.

In the meantime there are rulings Judge Fried needs to make before the following witness, the infamous Johnny Ding, is brought before the jury. "All right." The judge looks to the prosecutor. "Let's tick them off one at a time."

Leemie recites a "wish list" of Joe Chen's acts, all bad, that she wants to tell the jury in order to substantiate that he had a relationship with Johnny Ding. Just as she did earlier in the trial, Leemie cites a number of decisions, case law, to back up the reasons she should be allowed to include these items in the trial.

But Glenn has case law, too, to show why these items cannot be revealed. "I assume the source of this information about my client's bad acts is Johnny Ding." It is. "Is there independent evidence to support Johnny Ding's claims?" There is not.

According to Glenn, these acts are extremely prejudicial to his client. If the jury hears about any of them, they will presume that his client is a very bad man. And if his client is a very bad man, the jury could presume he is guilty of this kidnapping. The defense must resist this.

> **JUDGE FRIED SAYS:**
> In such evidentiary rulings, the court must balance the relevance of the information against the prejudicial effect on the jury.

Judge Fried will give them a ruling tomorrow morning.

LEEMIE'S WISH LIST:

Item I: Relationship with the Chinese gang called Tung On.

Joe Chen is not a member of Tung On, but he was present when some members, including Johnny Ding, took part in gang activities.

Leemie wants Johnny Ding to be allowed to talk about these activities.

Item II: Beatings and the murder.

Joe Chen and Johnny Ding took part in the beating of a rival gang member. Also, Joe Chen was present when Johnny Ding shot to death a member of another gang.

Item III: The Halloween night incident.

On Halloween night, 1994, Joe Chen took part in another kidnapping. Johnny Ding visited the crime apartment. That's why Johnny Ding decided to call him about the second victim, Mr. Li.

Item IV: Handcuffs.

Johnny Ding later committed his own kidnapping. He says that he learned where to buy handcuffs from Joe Chen.

GLENN'S RESPONSE:

Item I: Joe Chen isn't even *in* the gang. He was merely present at these gang incidents. He's not been charged with anything.

Item II: All the participants were from the same village in China. They grew up together. Therefore, it is not necessary to talk about gang-related incidents in the United States to show that they have a relationship. It's too prejudicial.

Item III: But Johnny Ding once kidnapped the defendant's brother, Sonny Chen. Joe Chen negotiated with Johnny Ding for his release. The significance of this act shows that the two men had dealings with each other regarding a kidnapping.

Besides, Johnny Ding's real relationship is with Jane Ding, who was living at the apartment. It was Johnny Ding who suggested to Jane Ding the kidnapping of Mr. Wang.

Item IV: The fact that the defendant told Johnny Ding where to get handcuffs has no relevance whatsoever.

. . .

AFTERNOON SESSION

Jane Ding finally arrives and is about to face Joe Chen's attorney. Leemie worries about her. "Jane is afraid. She is deathly afraid of Joe Chen, and she has no understanding of the legal system. At first she was even suspicious of me."

Just before the cross-examination, Judge Fried talks to the witness: "Ms. Ding, if you are asked a question that calls for a yes or no answer, just answer it 'yes' or 'no.' Don't volunteer information unless it's asked for. And if you do not understand the question, simply say that you do not understand the question." Jane nods.

"Proceed, Mr. Garber."

Glenn approaches the witness, his mind racing. He must impeach, or undermine, Jane Ding's direct testimony. After all, the defense contends, this woman is selling out her boyfriend's brother, who was also her friend, who was also her cousin-in-law, in order to get less time in jail.

> **IMPEACH:**
> To challenge the credibility or the validity of the testimony of a witness; to cast doubt on.

First question. "Is it your testimony that you were promised no money for the kidnapping?"

"What do you mean? I do not understand," says the witness.

Glenn rephrases.

She still does not understand. He asks again.

It does not take long for this cross-examination to get lost in a quagmire of words. The witness is infuriatingly vague. "What are you talking about?" she asks over and over again. She refuses to answer any of his questions. "I cannot answer the question because I do not know what you mean," she tells Glenn. He restates. "I don't understand." He rephrases. "I don't understand." He repeats.

"Huh?"

Nothing works.

Half an hour goes by. Then an hour. Then an hour and a half. The interpreter is becoming surly. Glenn's shirttail pulls out of his trousers. The jury is having a hard time following the line of questioning. Everybody is.

Glenn wets his lips. "Nobody promised you any money for your participation in this kidnapping, is that what you're saying?"

"No," she answers, wide-eyed.

Glenn pushes on, "Were you asked the following question at the grand jury proceeding?" He reads the question from the grand jury transcript, spitting out her answer, "Yes."

No reaction.

He moves to his next point, the fact that Jane Ding still owed a great deal of money for her smuggling fee. "You told the police officers you owed Johnny Ding $3,000, isn't that correct?"

> **JANE DING'S GRAND JURY TESTIMONY:**
> Question: "And were you promised some money, and did you, in fact, receive some money for participating in this kidnapping?"
> Answer: "Yes."

"It was not what *I* owed him. He requested that amount of money from my parents."

"So, you did *not* owe him $3,000. Is that what you are saying?" He is shouting.

"I did not say that," she shouts back.

Glenn wants to show the jury that this witness has a strong motive for placing the blame on his client. He focuses on her plea agreement with the district attorney's office. It's as if he were a dentist pulling teeth. Somehow, though, he manages to make a record of the following information: Jane was arrested on July 15, 1996. Her lawyer told her that if she went to trial she would possibly spend the rest of her life in jail. Rather than face trial, she pleaded guilty. Then she entered into an agreement with the district attorney's office.

Glenn asks about the plea agreement, but once again she doesn't understand his question. He speaks very slowly. "I — asked — you — whether — you — entered — into — an — agreement — with — the — district — attorney's — office. It calls for a yes or no answer."

"I do not understand."

Glenn demands, "You know this person over here?" And he points to the assistant district attorney, his voice rising higher and higher.

"Yes, I know her."

"What's her name?" he spouts.

"Lee Lee." Jurors giggle.

"Leemie Kahng, correct?"

"Yes."

He stops, head cocked, fighting laughter. "You call her Lee Lee?"

"I don't know. I never called her."

"Ha!" members of the jury burst out. Jane shifts in her seat; she is very tense.

Glenn yells again. "And the deal was that you can get as low as three years in jail if you cooperate?"

"I don't understand," she whispers. "Can I say something?"

"No," storms Glenn. He is pacing back and forth.

"I cannot answer your question because I do not know what you mean," she roars back.

Palms up, Glenn looks to the judge for help. "Can we approach for a second?"

"Let me see if I can clarify," says the judge.

Judge Fried believes that Jane is terrified because a wrong move with the defense could cost her the cooperation agreement. Jane answers the judge's questions about her plea agreement easily, yeses and noes, and they are able to move on.

By now the interpreter is absolutely exhausted and needs a break. The jury, too, is tired and noticeably confused. Not much has been accomplished. Almost everyone leaves the courtroom. Glenn continues pacing. He knows that he must impeach this witness. He senses that the cross is taking too long, he is losing the jury.

"Maybe I should mention that Jane Ding has a dragon tattoo on her arm?" he says, leaning toward me. A dragon tattoo is the symbol of the Green Dragons, another street gang in Chinatown. "But then that could leave open the fact that Joe Chen also has a dragon tattoo." He shakes his head. "Kahng is very thorough. She'll figure out some way to include it in the trial."

When the trial resumes, Glenn glances at his notes and moves on to the time when Jane Ding told the detectives that Johnny Ding was the dailo.

"Johnny Ding is a snake head, isn't that right?"

"That's right," she answers before the translator has a chance to tell her the question.

Glenn jumps at this. "You were nodding before I finished the question. Do you understand English?"

"I have been in jail for two years. I do know some."

"So you understood my question, right?" He hopes the jury sees that she is not as confused as she appears. Now he needs to show the jury that she will say anything to cut a better deal.

"After you gave information about Johnny Ding, he got arrested, right?"

"Possibly that was the case. I don't remember when."

"Up to this point, you did not say anything about Joe Chen's being involved in the kidnapping, correct?"

"Right."

"Now, all of a sudden, you are going to talk about Joe Chen?"

"Not all of a sudden, almost a year. I loved my boyfriend, Sonny Chen. That's why I waited almost a year. First time I talked to the police, I lied because of my boyfriend." Juror number one, a beautiful young woman, nods her head.

"You are now facing three years in jail." He's getting what he needs from her now—and Jane knows it. Leemie writes furiously on her legal pad.

"This is what I've been told. I don't believe it. All I know is my heart is not satisfied."

Forget "satisfied," Glenn says to himself; stay on the numbers. "Now your range is three to nine years, rather than six to eighteen years?"

"All I know, I have to tell all the truth. Maybe then they will give me three-to-nine. But why I'm here is not regarding three years. My heart is not satisfied because everybody was involved in this, and we are in here and he is out there in freedom."

Glenn asks if she lied to the police.

"At the beginning I didn't really lie. I only mentioned Johnny Ding. I didn't mention Joe Chen. Now, I am not lying."

"After you *lied* to them, you ended up with a better deal from the government." She shakes her head. He continues. "At some point it was explained to you that if you cooperate you can get as low as three-to-nine?"

"Yes." She repeats, "They told me I have to tell the truth."

Glenn tries hard to keep her on track. This is just what he needs to punch holes in her testimony. But Glenn has paid a price to reach this point. He is aggravated and exhausted. His once-ironed white shirt hangs crumpled from his trousers. "What I'm asking you about is the agreement that you have with *this* office." He points to Leemie again. Then he lowers his voice and walks toward the jury. "That is what I'm asking about. Maybe we can get through this. I'm not asking you about the truth right now." In a blink a tiny smile crosses the prosecutor's face. She writes his comment in big letters.

The judge corrects him. "I think that you mean that you are not ask-ing about the *facts*."

"Whatever," says Glenn, with a wave of his arm, anxious to finish this cross.

"There's a difference," the judge says gently.

Glenn realizes his mistake. "I'm not talking about her *reference* to the truth. I'm talking about the agreement."

Judge Fried addresses Jane. "Do you understand? He's asking you only about the agreement you have with the district attorney's office."

Jane looks over at the judge. "Can you tell him that I apologize because sometimes I don't understand the question?"

.   .   .

There is a ten-minute break. More pacing. "She's smart," says Glenn. "She answers the judge's questions, but plays dumb with me. On top of that, the translators act as a wedge between the witness and me."

He says, "Oh, this is a disaster. Jane Ding says that Joe Chen is free while the rest of the group are in jail. I could tell the jury that he is in jail, too, as another indication that she is a liar. But then they will see a crook for a defendant. I'm between a rock and a hard place. I have to figure out where to go with this. When the judge appears to agree with me, she straightens out. When he appears not to agree with me, she plays games. I must make the jury understand that she is a manipulator. She is manipulating everyone, including me."

.   .   .

After the break Glenn asks for a sidebar. He tells Judge Fried that when Jane Ding said that she did not implicate Joe Chen because she loved his brother, she was lying. She did incriminate him once before, for a number of burglaries. She also told the police that he was involved in gang activity. So much for family loyalty. But unless Glenn brings it before the jury, which, obviously, he doesn't want to do, they will not know these facts and there is nothing the judge can do about it.

By four-thirty Judge Fried has dismissed the jury. "Are we close?" a juror asks.

"We're not off schedule," the judge tells the group. "I anticipated there would be problems, so I built it into my schedule for you. So have a pleasant evening. See you tomorrow morning."

Never trusting the other side, Glenn asks that the judge instruct the assistant district attorney not to confer with Jane Ding about this part of her testimony.

Leemie is annoyed. She knows the rules, that she cannot talk to a witness during cross-examination.

. . .

Glenn sees that his confrontational style is getting him nowhere. "My frustration was becoming an issue in the trial," he later tells me. "I was too emotional." That night Glenn discussed his strategy with his wife. "She gave me insights. I should become removed and just get the facts out." He decides to be less sarcastic, less confrontational.

TIME: THURSDAY, APRIL 23, 1998; 9:30 A.M.
PLACE: THE COURTROOM

When Judge Fried enters the courtroom, he finds the two attorneys working pleasantly, side by side. The previous day's rancor is gone. Leemie looks spectacular in a long gray wool pleated skirt, gray jacket, black heels. Glenn is elegant in a charcoal-gray suit with a blue-and-white pin-striped shirt. Joe Chen sits ramrod straight, still wearing his gray suit and Statue of Liberty tie.

The judge is ready to rule on the four items, Leemie's wish list, that were discussed yesterday. "It seems to me," he says, "that most of the evidence of the defendant's bad acts is relevant." Glenn throws down his pencil and jerks his head forward in disbelief. Leemie does not move an inch. Judge Fried cites case law to explain his decision.

While Glenn is one very unhappy defense attorney, Joe Chen shows no reaction at all.

Once the trial resumes, Jane enters the courtroom wearing the same clothing as the day before. This time, though, she looks quite pale.

The defense attorney has questions about her boyfriend, Sonny Chen. When Jane continues to dodge, Glenn softly asks, "Miss Ding, is it the exact words that you are confused with?"

"I don't understand what you are talking about," she replies.

"Now, when Ms. Kahng was asking you questions, you didn't have much difficulty answering those questions, did you?" He tilts his head.

"Not right," she counters brusquely.

"Your Honor..." Glenn groans.

The judge talks directly to Jane: "The way we conduct a trial is that you are asked a question and then you answer the question. At a later point you may have an opportunity to explain. But an explanation at this time is not being asked for. Do you understand that?"

"I understand. What you are saying is that one day you are going to give me a chance to explain my answer." Not quite. The witness will be allowed to explain her answers only if the assistant district attorney decides her explanation is important for the jury to know.

· · ·

At long last Jane testifies that after the kidnapping she moved to a cousin's apartment. Under interrogation she told the police that her cousin was, instead, her sister.

"Can I explain what I meant?" she asks for the umpteenth time.

"Tell me what you meant," Glenn says magnanimously.

Judge Fried reminds her, "You can only explain if Mr. Garber allows you to explain. You can't explain it on your own."

Jane asks, "Did he say it's okay?"

Glenn, with a big, fatherly smile, says, "I said it was okay."

"You know, among our Fukinese, we don't really call cousin, first cousin, second cousin. We just call sisters or brothers. When I went to jail, the other inmates explained that my father's brother's daughter is my cousin, not my sister."

"Is this a good time to break, Mr. Garber?" asks the judge.

"This is fine."

"Have a nice lunch, ladies and gentlemen. Please do not discuss this case among yourselves."

AFTERNOON SESSION

Glenn changes his tactics once again. Speaking in rapid-fire, staccato sentences, he asks about Johnny Ding. Does she like him? Does she hate him?

"I hate him because he asked my parents for money when I first came to the United States. He called my parents and asked for $3,000."

What about Mr. Wang, the first victim? "We were only casual friends."

"You were married to Joe Chen's first cousin. Are you still married to him?"

"When we got married, we didn't sign the paper [marriage certificate]."

He quickly changes the subject. "Do you trust the district attorney's office?"

"Now I don't trust nobody."

He changes again. "When Sonny Chen and you became boyfriend-girlfriend, the defendant was very angry."

"Objection!" calls the prosecutor.

Sidebar!

Leemie does not see the relevance of these questions. The defense lawyer says that it "goes to motive to lie against my client." Judge Fried agrees with the defense. Objection overruled.

"Does Joe Chen's anger affect your relation with him?"

"Possibly yes." That's the answer the defense attorney is looking for. Throughout this ordeal, Glenn has kept one eye on the jury. He thinks that they do not believe this witness, so he puts everyone out of their misery.

"No further questions."

REDIRECT

In a flash Leemie is up. Before going to trial, Leemie interviewed Jane about her relationship with Sonny Chen. "She was devoted to the defendant's brother, really in love with him. It's sort of like a *True Romance* story when you talk to her," Leemie tells me after the trial. Leemie asks the witness why she did not immediately tell the police about Joe Chen.

"Because of his younger brother, Sonny Chen," Jane says.

"But then why did you eventually decide to tell about Joe Chen?" Leemie asks.

One day I realized they were using me. I was in prison for two years. Joe Chen came to the prison and visited me once. He sent me fifty dollars. He told me not to say anything. In my heart nobody can tell me whether— what I should say, what I not to say.

On the first day I entered the prison, I wanted to tell, but I didn't, only because I loved his younger brother. After I pleaded guilty, I called Joe Chen. I wanted him to give me a ten-dollar phone card so I can call China and talk to my parents. I was in prison for almost one year, and I didn't ask for anything. All I knew was I loved my boyfriend. I can give myself up for him. But later on I gave more thought that I only loved his younger brother, why should I give myself up for Joe Chen.

I talked to my boyfriend on the phone only once. I told him, I said, "I love you. I can do anything for you." Even though at that time I didn't want to plead guilty. He begged me. He said to me—

"Objection!"

"Sustained."

Jane is crying.

Glenn asks to approach the bench again. He objects to this line of questioning. And once again Leemie is ready for him. "Judge, she was pretty well instructed to answer either 'yes' or 'no' on cross-examination, and I thought it only fair that she be entitled to give an explanation about her answers during cross-examination."

"Objection overruled."

The prosecutor asks one final question. "Miss Ding, is that why you did not tell about Joe Chen at first?"

"Yes."

Leemie has no further questions.

RECROSS

Glenn asks if it is just a coincidence that Jane changed her story after she heard about the new deal for a lower sentence. "I don't pay any concern to these," she replies to Glenn's questions.

Then, surprisingly, she becomes a chatterbox, describing elaborate, alternative sentencing agreements. Glenn does not stop her. Her response easily implies that she knows the law, she knows what she is doing, and that she set up Joe Chen to get less time in prison. He's already proved that she is willing to lie, so the defense has no further questions.

REDIRECT AGAIN

Leemie must undo this last testimony. She asks questions to undercut Glenn's cross-examination that Jane would implicate the defendant to get less time. As always, Glenn listens carefully to Leemie's every word.

"Did you ever think you could get less than six years?"

"No."

"And it wasn't until after Joe Chen was arrested that you were approached about testifying against him. Isn't that true?"

"Objection!" roars Glenn, pouncing on the word "after." He rushes to the sidebar and tells the judge, "I move for a mistrial."

ONE TINY WORD

Glenn has based much of his cross-examination on the fact that both Jane Ding and the next witness (Johnny Ding) told law enforcement there was another kidnapper so that they could get lighter sentences. Then Joe Chen was arrested.

"I specifically made a request for information about the timing of the cooperation agreement," Glenn tells the judge. Remember, the government must give the defense all the evidence prior to the trial. Otherwise, the defendant's attorney cannot prepare a rigorous defense. Now, this simple word, "after," could make or break the case. Glenn's face is bright red, his arms wave in the air.

If Joe was arrested because Jane and Johnny fingered him, Leemie's question makes no sense. But if Joe was arrested, and then Jane accused him *after,* that should have showed up in the records. Misinformation, or information unduly withheld, could be grounds to end the trial. That one word could make all Leemie's preparations, all the witnesses, all the evidence, go by the board.

Surprisingly, Leemie is not worried. She does not think a mistrial will be granted. Later she says, "I think Glenn legitimately thought he had grounds for a mistrial. Defense attorneys ask for a mistrial a lot when something happens that they believe prejudices their client in front of the jury."

Jury members strain their necks, fascinated, even though they can't hear anything. Joe Chen stares straight ahead as if nothing was happening.

Leemie is very careful. There was a period before the trial when she and her superior, Carla Freedman, chief of the Asian Gang Unit, had a number of conversations with Jane Ding. "I wasn't clear about what exact date she actually implicated him."

She tells the judge, "My question was based on the assumption that we would never talk about a cooperation agreement before a person is arrested. We talk about it after the arrest."

The judge calmly mediates. He will not grant a mistrial. Then they would have to start all over again, or Joe Chen could go free. He settles on a compromise: Leemie will withdraw the question. The jury will disregard this testimony. Glenn will keep his theory in play. No mistrial.

Back to open court. Glenn is not smiling. The judge instructs the jury to disregard the last question. Once again the jury is asked to follow the rules of the law, not what they heard. In effect the judge is saying, "You did not hear that," even though they did.

"Anything further?" asks the judge.

"No," says Leemie. Glenn has nothing more. The witness, Jane Ding, is finally excused.

. . .

Although it's been a tough battle, Glenn was able to show that Jane Ding has a strong motive to lie about Joe Chen. But this victory comes with a heavy price: the jury became restless, confused, and impatient. A lawyer cannot afford to lose the attention of a jury. Glenn may have won the battle, but did he lose the war?

JOHNNY DING AND COMPANY

- LEEMIE CALLS JOHNNY DING, A SECOND COOPERATING WITNESS, TO THE STAND. HE TELLS ABOUT HIS LIFE AS A TUNG ON GANG MEMBER.
- JOHNNY DING SAYS THAT JOE CHEN IS THE LEADER OF THE KIDNAPPERS.

TIME: FRIDAY, APRIL 24, 1998; 9:45 A.M.
PLACE: JUDGE FRIED'S COURTROOM

Johnny Ding. Jurors eye each other in recognition of the name. This is the person they have been waiting for, the snake head murderer who was first mentioned at the beginning of the trial. But the young man who sits in the witness box, in a gray business suit, starched white shirt, and maroon-and-blue striped tie, doesn't look at all like a cutthroat thug. He's more like a young professional, an accountant perhaps, or an investment banker, or maybe even a lawyer.

Later, Leemie explained why she put Johnny Ding on the stand. "It is always good to have more witnesses, especially when they corroborate each other. I knew that he was not an entirely sympathetic character, but I thought it was instrumental to develop how the kidnapping was planned and how it unfolded."

. . .

"I am thirty years old this year," Johnny tells the court in response to Leemie's question. "I speak Fuchow [sic]. I understand a little Mandarin. I went up to middle school in China. I was in a car business in China. I transported customers. Jane Ding was my next-door neighbor. I consider her my older sister. When her family had a banquet or party, our family would attend. Many generations ago we were related, we came from the same ancestor."

In March 1993, Johnny Ding made a deal with a snake head. He would pay more than $31,000 to be smuggled to America. "At that time I didn't have much to do in China. I thought I would do better in the United States." He left his wife and two small children to find riches and adventure in America.

His trip was similar to the one his neighbor, Jane Ding, would later take: a long ship ride to Mexico and a dangerous trek over the mountains to California. "When we got to the border we ran across. I got caught in San Diego. I was held for seventeen days. I do not know which method the snake heads used to get me out on bail."

Johnny was put on a plane to New York, picked up at the other end by new snake heads, and taken to a safe house. Sometimes the snake head would add fees, expenses for room (a cellar floor) and board (meager meals). "My family could not come up with that large sum of U.S. dollars. I was held for six months until they got the money straight."

Johnny was kept in a basement with about a hundred other people. "I was often beaten up by the snake heads because I didn't have the money to pay them. Wintertime, they sprinkled cold water on us and then threw us out into the snow. That was the way to force us to pay. I called home, crying, quite a few times," he says, his eyes filling with tears. "I'm sorry. I get very emotional when I talk about this."

When Johnny was finally freed, friends picked him up in Chinatown and drove him to Albany. "I worked in Albany for about two months. I washed dishes and did odds and ends. Normally I worked from eleven A.M. to ten P.M. Then I moved to Baltimore because I knew people there from my village. I called them and asked if there were jobs. I worked in Baltimore for about two months, also washing dishes and doing odds and ends."

Washing dishes was not what Johnny Ding had in mind when he came to America. One night he telephoned a friend in New York. This friend was a member of a Chinese gang, the Tung On. "Why don't you come here?" the friend suggested.

"I told him I was afraid to hang around with him. I still owed money. He said, 'If you hang around with us, you don't have to be afraid because we control the entire street.'"

Johnny still owed his family twelve thousand dollars. "I was working and my salary wasn't high, so I quit my job and came to New York. I joined the Tung On gang."

In May 1994, when Johnny Ding joined Tung On, they were involved in operating gambling parlors, extorting local merchants, and guarding massage parlors. "Basically we gang members were told to watch these places and keep other gangs away."

Leemie questions Johnny further about his life as a soldier in the Tung Ons.

Oh, I was one of the brothers. I followed the daima [the second in command, the lieutenant, under the dailo]. I collected street extortion and watched gambling parlors. When there were fights on the street, I would take part. I had to protect a massage parlor so that it wasn't robbed by others.

We only collected from Chinese businesses, because they knew less

English and were afraid of the police. We never collected from Americans, because they would report it to the police.

If Chinese businessmen would not give money, we ransacked their stores. Every day we had a group of people hanging around the front of the store so customers were not able to go in. They were afraid. The store-keepers were losing business, so they paid us money every month.

The gang had already established a history of extortion when I came. All the dailo had to do is tell the daima to get money from a business. I'm not sure about how much money was collected because that was controlled by someone higher up. The bigger stores paid in the high hundreds.

I was like a soldier, meaning I followed them. There were fights in the streets. We would go into apartments and take things. We took things from people on the streets. No one would dare to say anything.

Basically, I stayed at a gambling parlor on East Broadway. I took part in many fights, two robberies, and a few extortions. I also participated in robbing a massage parlor that belonged to Jane Ding's uncle.

Normally we only showed our knives because everyone was already aware of us—afraid of us. We didn't dare bring our guns because the police were on the streets. We were often searched by them.

Later I got involved in smuggling. I became a snake head. In the beginning, though, I wasn't involved in that. It was after I was hanging out in the street . . . a person . . . Joe Chen—

"Come to the side a minute," Judge Fried says quickly, interrupting the testimony. "What is this turning into?" the judge asks.

"Nothing, judge, I didn't mean to elicit that," Leemie explains. "I tried to prep him. I explained there are only two things he can talk about, the things that you ruled on earlier." Remember, Leemie may ask if Joe Chen hung out with the Tung Ons when they were involved in gang-related activity, but she may not ask about specific criminal activities. "I didn't know that my question was going to elicit that response."

Back in open court, the judge tells the jury to disregard the last answer. "It plays no part in this trial." The jury leaves the courtroom while Leemie reinstructs the witness.

As soon as the jury leaves, Glenn protests. "Right after he talked about the smuggling, he mentioned my client's name. I move for a mistrial."

"I heard exactly what he said, and I'm denying your application."

·   ·   ·

Later Judge Fried explains his ruling: "The witness was involved in certain criminal activities with the defendant that I will not allow the jury to hear. I became concerned that he might blurt out this information. When that happens it is difficult to pull back. When Johnny Ding specifically said 'smuggling,' I was worried that he would say something else.

"After Ms. Kahng talked to the witness, I told him, 'Do not volunteer any information, just answer the question.' I was still worried that he might say something specific and then I would have a problem." If Johnny Ding mentions specific bad acts that Joe Chen may have committed, this could prejudice the jury and indeed lead to a mistrial.

Once the jurors return, Judge Fried allows Leemie to lead the witness. She questions him about Tung On gang activities, including beatings and extortions.

> **LEADING THE WITNESS:**
> In certain situations, a lawyer may ask the judge for permission to lead the witness during direct examination by asking questions to be answered either "yes" or "no."

Finally she asks one last leading question. "And, Mr. Ding, during the summer of 1994, did you shoot and kill somebody?"

"Yes."

"Can you explain to the jury the circumstances of that shooting?" Members of the jury lean forward.

THE STORY OF KIT AND ACER

At that time there was a person called Kit. Kit's level in Tung On was the same as my dailo, whose name is Acer. Kit and Acer have had a battle for more than ten years.

Finally Kit called for a truce and he handed over his power to Acer. We soldiers of both dailos worked together, robbing people of watches and cellular phones. After one robbery, we tried to settle our interests. Our gang members were not happy with the distribution, so we beat up Kit's gang members.

Kit called Acer to ask why this happened. Both leaders decided that it was better for them to stick together than continue fighting. We all went out for a dinner as a way to make amends and celebrate our continuing friendship.

At the dinner everyone got drunk. Once again, our gang beat up Kit's gang. Kit said, "If this is the case, you guys do not like me anymore. I will go independent. I will set up another Tung On branch. We will settle this in the street."

Acer worried that the other side would have more power than our group and he ordered us to kidnap Kit. We held him at one of the massage parlors that was in our control. We beat Kit's legs with metal sticks. We beat him and beat him until he became unconscious. Then we threw him out into the street. A police car came by, picked him up, and took him to the hospital.

When Kit was released from the hospital, he vowed revenge. Kit's men raided our massage parlor and beat up everyone who was inside, including Acer's brother-in-law. Acer knew he had to force Kit's group off the street. To do this we needed help. We contacted outsiders, friends who were loyal. Acer had lots of friends.

There were many fights, many beatings. At first we used metal sticks.
Then we moved to guns.

On August 7, 1996, I was ordered to shoot a member of the other side.
It happened in a telephone booth, on East Broadway—

"Objection," shouts Glenn. He and the prosecutor approach the
bench. Leemie anticipates Glenn's objection. "I know. Mr. Garber is
worried because he thinks that something about his client might come
out. But there were two other people involved, as far as I know, and at
least one other person had a gun. It was basically just a barrage of
shooting."

The judge asks, "What is the relevance of whether other people
were involved?"

She replies, "Just the circumstances of what the shooting was like."

"I'm not going to allow it. The fact that he shot somebody, whether
in concert with other people or not, is irrelevant. I'm concerned that
when you say 'in concert with other people,' you may create a situation
where the jury could infer it was this defendant." Indeed, Joe Chen was
at the scene of the crime, but he did not participate. They return to
open court, and Leemie jumps ahead and asks Johnny what happened
after the murder.

I got rid of the gun. After the shooting I took a car and went to Forty-
second Street and then returned to my friend's home. After a few days I
returned to the gang.

I went to Baltimore and hid there. I was in Baltimore about ten
months. I hid in my friend's home and waited for my company to tell me
everything was okay. After 1995, I watched over a gambling hall.

Leemie moves on to June 1997, when Johnny was arrested. At first
he was placed in pretrial detention. Then, in July, he was taken into

federal custody, where he remains incarcerated. Two months after his arrest, Johnny entered into a cooperative agreement with the federal authorities.

Johnny squirms in his seat while he explains the terms of his federal agreement. "My cooperation agreement says zero to life. And I must also give up the right to fight deportation.

"The facts are as I stated. I cannot lie. I have to tell the full truth. If I lie, I don't be able to get a good night's sleep. I did a bad thing that will always be in my mind. I do not know what punishment they are going to give me, but at least I may have a chance to start a new life."

Johnny understands that a United States attorney will write a letter that recommends a particular sentence. It is up to a federal judge to sentence him. This judge can sentence him to life in prison, less, much less, or even free him of the charge.

"I feel in my own heart that I must testify," he tells the jury. A dramatic time to break for lunch.

LUNCH BREAK

After lunch Judge Fried instructs the jury about the testimony they are about to hear. "I charge you that I'm only allowing this evidence in for the limited purpose of explaining—if you choose to believe the evidence—the background relationship between this defendant and the witness, and for no other purpose. Continue, please."

Leemie sets the scene by asking about the kidnapping. "And Mr. Ding," asks Leemie, "during the summer of 1995, were you in Baltimore?"

"Yes."

"And did there come a time when you took a bus from Baltimore to New York City in August of 1995?"

> **JUDGE FRIED'S INSTRUCTION TO THE JURY:**
> Ladies and gentleman, the fact I'm receiving this testimony in evidence is no proof whatsoever that the defendant, Mr. Joe Chen, possessed any propensity or disposition to commit any crime, or any other crime that is not charged in this indictment, and it may not be considered by you for that purpose.

"Yes."

Johnny Ding and Mr. Li, the second victim, once worked together in a restaurant. By chance, Johnny sees Mr. Li at the bus station.

"During this bus ride, did you decide that you were going to bring this man to an apartment?" questions Leemie.

"It was during the bus trip I made the decision."

"But this is not anything you had planned before you got to the bus station?"

"No."

"And did there come a time that you made any phone calls?"

"Yes."

"Where from?"

"Grand Central Station. I lied to the individual and told him to wait for a few minutes."

"Who did you call when you made that phone call?"

"Joe Chen." As usual, when the defendant's name is mentioned, the jurors look at him for some reaction. No reaction. Leemie continues to question.

"What was your conversation during that call?"

"I said I have an individual. He doesn't know much about New York. Do you have a place where we can hold him? His answer was yes, he has a place. And he told me that he already has a person there. He told me if I can wait for a few minutes he'll send somebody to come out and lead me to his place. A few minutes later Cow Eyes showed up."

The prosecutor asks for a sidebar. She tells the judge that she is now going to question the witness about item III, the Halloween incident. This is the episode where Joe Chen took part in a different kidnapping, and Johnny visited the apartment where the victim was being held.

Judge Fried tells the prosecutor to lead the witness, as a safety precaution. Back in open court the judge reminds the jury about the instruction he gave when the jury returned from lunch. Glenn's hand tightens around his pencil. He and Joe Chen stare straight ahead. There is nothing they can do about the following testimony—at least not now.

Leemie asks, "Mr. Ding, on or about Halloween, 1994, in an apartment in Brooklyn, did you see the defendant holding another individual in that apartment, yes or no?"

"Yes."

"Was that incident one that you were involved with, yes or no?"

"No."

"Was that why you called Joe Chen in August 1995?"

"Yes."

She quickly changes the subject. "Did Cow Eyes bring you to an apartment eventually?" Glenn lets out a quiet sigh.

"Luke Chen—Cow Eyes, yes."

"Had you ever been to that apartment?"

"No."

"What happened when you got inside the apartment?"

"Joe and Sonny Chen were waiting in the apartment. I walked in with the individual. Right after we entered the room, Joe said, 'Tie him up.' Then Cow Eyes and Sonny tied him up like this." Johnny puts both his arms behind his back and continues, "The victim yelled my other name, 'Charlie Chan! Charlie Chan!' I didn't want to answer him. And then I heard Cow Eyes and other people speak to him, saying if you keep screaming we'll beat you to death. And then a little bit later, he stopped screaming.

"They used clothes to blindfold him and they threw him into a room. Then they brought in another victim and they tied them together.

"Joe Chen told Cow Eyes to beat him. After Cow Eyes beat him up, he shut up. Sonny Chen joined the beatings too. Stick, another guy, came later and beat him too."

Leemie asks, "What did you, Sonny, Joe, and Cow Eyes say to the victim?"

"We said to get the money as soon as possible, or we will beat you to death. If you don't get the money by the due date, we will beat you to death. He was scared."

"Did you also beat the victim?"

"Yes. Then he gave us his family's phone number."

"What happened then?"

"Joe Chen and I made phone calls to his family. We said if you want to see your relative, you must get the money ready. If you don't want your relative, then he will disappear."

In continuing testimony Johnny Ding tells the court that both he and Joe Chen made all the phone calls. They used a regular phone and a cell phone. Johnny's fee for the kidnapping was $3,000.

Johnny beat both victims during their days spent in captivity. He put a gun to their heads, taunting them, threatening them. Stick, who has not been apprehended, beat the victims as well. Johnny Ding says, "My victim, Mr. Li, told my girlfriend that he was tricked by me. He talked too much and I got very angry with him. I kicked him. I didn't want my girlfriend to find out and fight with me."

Leemie asks, "After this kidnapping, you then committed your own kidnapping with two other people?"

"Correct." Another crime to add to the list.

"In the same apartment?"

"Correct."

"But it had nothing to do with Joe Chen, Sonny Chen, and Cow Eyes?"

"Right."

"How many people did you kidnap at that time?"

"Three. I made over ten thousand."

After the second kidnapping, Johnny tells the jury that he went back to his old job, watching the gambling parlor. He worked there until the day he was arrested. No further questions.

After this direct examination Leemie is not sure what kind of impression Johnny Ding made on the jury.

As Glenn prepares to cross-examine the witness, he says, "I think I should change my approach with Johnny Ding. I'll become very dead-pan. I'm sick of fighting with the interpreters. I think they took my aggressive cross of Jane Ding personally. Maybe if I am mellow, they will be more cooperative."

IS THIS THE TRUTH?

- GLENN CROSS-EXAMINES JOHNNY DING ABOUT HIS UNSAVORY PAST.
- JOHNNY DING EXPLAINS HIS AGREEMENTS WITH THE STATE AND FEDERAL COURTS.

TIME: FRIDAY, APRIL 24, 1998; 3;30 P.M.
PLACE: JUDGE FRIED'S COURTROOM

Glenn takes a quick glance at his notes while Johnny Ding waits passively in the witness box. Facing the jury rather than the witness, he asks the following questions:

"In 1994, you shot and killed somebody."

"Correct."

"With a gun?"

"Correct."

"The bullet hit his head?"

"It was such confusion. We shot, we fired, and all I know, he is dead. I have been told by the law officers that he's dead."

"You beat people?"

"I did."

"With metal bars?"

"Correct."

"You extorted store owners?"

"Correct."

"You threatened them?"

"Yes."

"And it was your goal to keep these people in fear, isn't that correct?"

"Right."

"So that your gang could thrive?"

"Yes."

"And when you killed this man, it advanced your position in the gang." Pause. "Correct?"

"That was an order from above."

"That compliance advanced your position in the gang?"

"That's correct."

Glenn is deadpan. It's as if he was asking: "You bought the tomatoes?...Right?...And carrots?...Correct?..."

Suddenly Glenn spins around and faces the witness. "You approached another man and punched him? You pulled a knife on him and demanded $1,800." He is angry. He needs to be angry. It is appropriate to be angry. "This person is screwing my client," he later explains. "A jury would not have the energy to acquit Joe if I wasn't outraged at his accusers."

Glenn becomes a bombardier, diving in for the kill. "The man ran away....You ran after him....You grabbed him and threatened to kill him if he didn't pay the money."

"That didn't happen," Johnny screams back.

Louder and louder. "And you threatened him—"

"… We had an argument. It was a back-and-forth argument. It was a dispute between brothers."

Glenn turns back to the jury and serenely asks, "So it's a lie when they charged you for that particular crime?"

"When that charge was brought against me, it was a dispute between brothers. The brother didn't come back to accuse me." Johnny fidgets, but only a little.

"You threatened to cut off his fingers in that case, didn't you?" Glenn says, reminding the jury that someone bragged about cutting off Mr. Li's finger. (Earlier in the trial, Mr. Wang said that someone whom he could not identify told him that the second victim's finger had been cut off. *His finger—one of his fingers had already been cut off. And he waved it in front of me.* Leemie's theory is that the unidentified person was Joe Chen. Glenn believes it was Johnny Ding.)

"That was not what I said. I threatened him on the phone. I said, 'If you don't give the money, then you will be beaten up. You will be hit in the leg.' "

Glenn asks about even more crimes: three other kidnappings, a few beatings, and a robbery at Jane Ding's uncle's massage parlor.

Glenn tilts his head; his eyes widen. "You have committed all these crimes, and all of a sudden, you want to come clean? Is that your testimony?"

Johnny replies, "Someone who committed crimes, someone who did wrong, knows it very well in their heart. When they do something wrong in the past, they can't even sleep well at night. It is like jail, jail within your mind. When I got arrested by the police, I thought back to all the pain that I caused my victims. Because for the sake of money, I did these things to hurt—"

"But now?" Glenn interrupts. He wants the jury to hear this.

"I feel that in my heart—"

The defense lawyer breaks in. "Mr. Johnny Ding, this transformation that you are talking about occurred *after* you got arrested and were held in jail?"

"When I think back, I realize I hurt these people—"

Glenn begins the sentence, "You are facing—"

"I have to face the truth of what I did," the witness inserts.

"—You are facing a life sentence in a federal prison. Correct?"

"Myself, whatever punishment they are going to impose on me—I did so many bad things to other people—I have to tell all the truth. I have to come clean." He rocks back and forth. "Whatever time is left after prison, I will have a second chance. Start fresh. It doesn't matter to me anymore now. Today I'm here, I'm here to take the stand because it's actually—I'm trying to rescue my own brother [Joe Chen] not to do any more crime to any other innocent people. If you harm innocent people, you harm yourself, too."

The witness calms down and looks directly at the jurors and says, "If you help him escape from punishment, he will go do more harm to other innocent people."

Glenn allows the oration because he does not think the jury believes this witness. But just to be certain, he creates a trap for the newly virtuous Johnny Ding. Like a spider out to catch a fly, Glenn spins a web of questions. "And you're being very honest with the government, correct?" he asks simply.

"Of course. I have to tell the truth," says the unsuspecting witness.

"That's exactly the right thing to do. Does that make your heart feel better?" Glenn asks. His voice is soft, luring his prey deeper into his trap.

"I feel more calm now. It's not that I want revenge, I just want to make that clear, whatever they did. . . ."

Leemie sees what's happening and objects. Judge Fried overrules her.

Glenn adds a new strand to the web. "You are saying you got $3,000 for this kidnapping?" No response. Glenn asks, "Correct?" Still no response.

"Correct?" asks Glenn, louder.

"Correct," the witness whispers.

"Is this difficult for you?" the defense attorney asks.

"Yes, I received $3,000," he says, his voice strong.

Glenn moves to Johnny's federal agreement. "You spoke to the federal prosecutor. Is that right?"

Johnny repeats, "He told me if I tell the truth he will not bring charges against me. But I have to tell the truth. I told the truth."

Glenn springs his trap. "But you told the assistant U.S. attorney that you didn't get any money from this kidnapping. Correct?"

"Correct," Johnny admits. He lied.

Johnny tries hard to explain. "I only told him this case is in the state court. He said if it's in the state court, okay."

Glenn leans back. One trap in, now on to the next: "You're very aware of the difference between federal and state court, correct?"

JUDGE FRIED EXPLAINS FEDERAL AND STATE SENTENCING GUIDELINES:

Johnny Ding's cases are in two different jurisdictions—federal and state. The federal and state courts each operate under sentencing guidelines. Sentencing is different in every state in the country, and then again it is different from the federal courts.

I. Federal guidelines state that a cooperation agreement permits the United States attorney (the federal prosecutor) great discretion. If the prosecutor believes that cooperation is substantial, then the cooperator will receive a 5.K.1. letter [5.K.1. simply refers to section 5, paragraph K, subdivision 1 of the relevant statute].

A 5.K.1. letter means that the federal judge is no longer bound by sentencing guidelines. The judge's sentence can even be no time in prison.

Johnny Ding doesn't have the 5.K.1. yet. He is hoping to get it. It is entirely up to the federal judge to sentence him to anywhere from zero to life in prison.

II. Tying into this is Johnny Ding's state agreement. A New York State judge cannot sentence a cooperator below the minimum demand of the law, even if his information is the most valuable evidence for law enforcement. Johnny Ding pleaded guilty to two counts of kidnapping in the second degree. Under the required state sentencing laws this crime has a mandatory minimum of two to six years, maximum eight and a third to twenty-five years.

If Johnny Ding ends up with more time from the federal court than he gets from the state court, the judge in the state can run his sentence concurrently [simultaneously]. If, on the other hand, he is given less time from the federal court, he will serve more years from the state court, with either a concurrent or a consecutive [one after the other] sentence.

"Yeah, of course. Case here and over there. It's different."

"You know you can get any sentence by the judge in the federal court?"

"I will ask the judge if they give me another chance, I will start to begin a fresh person and new person. If they don't give me a chance, I will be in jail my whole life. I can't think of this thing, it's not up to me."

"For killing somebody..." Glenn looks over toward the jurors while Johnny answers.

"Right."

"...You're going to get a tremendous amount of time, or you're going to get a tremendous amount of time taken off your sentence for your cooperation."

Over the prosecutor's objection, he answers, "That's right."

Glenn moves on to the state sentencing for this crime, the double kidnapping. Before Johnny pleaded guilty, he was facing fifty years to life in prison if the judge sentenced him consecutively for the two kidnappings. But he worked out a deal with the prosecutor's office that would reduce his time to ten to thirty years in prison.

Johnny says, "That's up to the judge. I cannot make a decision for him." What happens is Leemie, the assistant district attorney, makes a recommendation to the judge about the length of time this witness should serve. The judge makes the final decision.

This is a dramatic place for the defense to stop for the day. So many crimes, and a chance for a lighter sentence, as low as ten years—strong motive indeed to put the blame on someone else. There are no further questions and the jury is dismissed. The witness is escorted out of the courtroom by three armed police officers.

Judge Fried says to Glenn, "I congratulate you on being able to effectively cross-examine the witness in fifteen minutes.

"Have a nice weekend."

TIME: MONDAY. APRIL 27. 1998. 9:00 A.M.
PLACE: JUDGE FRIED'S COURTROOM

Just before court is in session, Glenn leans over to the prosecutor's table and sweetly asks, "Leemie, did you put a plant in jail with Joe Chen over the weekend?" Since it is not illegal to put an informant in a cell with a defendant, Leemie might admit to it. Glenn wants to see Leemie's reaction.

"No!" she says.

"You know what I mean by a plant?" he needles her.

"I know. I know. I didn't do that."

In spite of last Friday's strong cross-examination, Glenn says that he feels like a beleaguered warrior. He worked on the case all weekend long. His two small children and his wife, who says she is ready to kill him, all had colds. Glenn was no help at all. At this point in time only the trial matters. Glenn says, "I can't worry about my family. I can't worry about anything other than my client. This is a very aggressive prosecution. Leemie seems to have covered every base."

"Coming in!" shouts a guard as he leads Joe Chen into the courtroom.

The jurors are present and waiting outside the courtroom. Joe Chen's handcuffs are removed, and the guard stands behind him. "Jury entering!" shouts another guard.

Johnny Ding enters the witness box, and Judge Fried reminds him that he is still under oath.

Glenn quickly moves on to another motive for Johnny's accusation against Joe Chen. This one has to do with the defendant's brother, Sonny.

Remember, Johnny Ding was one of the snake heads who smuggled Sonny Chen to America. But after he arrived, the Chen family back in China could not afford to pay all of the smuggling fees. Joe Chen asked Johnny Ding to help his brother.

Johnny explains, "I made phone calls. I spoke to snake heads in

Washington to see if he could be released with a $5,000 guarantee." As a favor to Johnny, the Washington snake heads lowered the fee. But the Chen family was still unable to pay. Johnny Ding vouched for him and Sonny was released. Another favor.

Some time later, Sonny Chen was kidnapped. Instead of calling Johnny Ding, Joe Chen reported it to the police. When Johnny heard that, he felt betrayed.

At that time there was a birthday party for Johnny at a Chinese restaurant. Joe Chen showed up and the two got into an argument. Joe Chen hit him.

Poor Johnny. He goes out of his way to help a friend and what did he get for it? A betrayal and a punch in the nose. And on his birthday yet. According to Glenn, an easy revenge would be fingering Joe Chen in this kidnapping.

Glenn moves on to this witness's behavior after his arrest. Johnny says, "When I first got arrested, I was trying to protect myself. I tried to lessen my participation. But after I started cooperation, I told them the full truth." He takes a sip of water from a plastic cup. "They asked if I knew Jane Ding," he tells the jury. "As soon as they asked me that name, I knew I couldn't get away with it. They also asked me about Sonny Chen and about Cow Eyes."

Johnny signed a statement confessing that he took part in the kidnapping. But he never mentioned beating the victims. As a matter of fact, he blamed the beatings on the other people. "I was trying to avoid problems for myself," he says. Leemie takes notes.

After he kidnapped the second victim, Johnny moved into the apartment on Rivington Street with the victims. But he lied again. He told the police that he only had a few drinks there and then left. "I was very nervous at the time," Johnny explains. "I was scared. I didn't know what answers I should give. I gave them the names of everyone who partici-pated. I gave them the truth about that."

The defense has no further questions.

.   .   .

Leemie heads straight to the witness. "Just to clarify, Mr. Ding, when you were questioned by the police, is it your testimony that you named all the participants in the crime, including the defendant?"

"Correct."

"Okay. But you minimized your own behavior because you were protecting yourself at that time?"

"Yes."

"Was there any talk about a deal at that time?"

"No. No."

"I have no further questions."

The judge asks if there are further questions from the defense.

"No."

The judge says, "Mr. Ding, you are excused. Thank you." Johnny Ding leaves the witness stand and returns to federal prison to await his fate.

Glenn leans back in his seat, one hand resting comfortably on Joe Chen's shoulder. He is feeling confident now that the jury could not possibly believe Johnny Ding.

ECHO

- CORROBORATING WITNESSES: LEEMIE TAKES THE TESTIMONY OF DETECTIVES, A TELEPHONE COMPANY INVESTIGATOR, AND A NEW WITNESS TO SUPPORT THE TESTIMONY OF HER COOPERATING WITNESSES.
- GLENN TRIES TO PROVE THAT LEEMIE'S EVIDENCE IS NOT STRONG ENOUGH TO CONVICT JOE CHEN.

In New York State, the testimony of an accomplice must be corroborated. That means there must be independent evidence connecting the defendant with the charge. One afternoon in a Malaysian restaurant in Chinatown, Judge Fried described how the corroboration rule works. "Let's say I am walking down the street and somebody steals my wallet. I point him out to the police. When the officer stops him, I say, 'This is the man.' You either believe me or you do not believe me. There is no need to corroborate because I have no particular reason to finger an innocent person.

"If, on the other hand, two people rob me. The police arrest one, but the other one gets away. Then the arrested fellow says that he will tell who was with him in return for a lighter sentence; he will cooperate. A deal is made, and the man says, 'Smith was with me.' The police arrest

Smith. The first man testifies against Smith. That testimony must be corroborated because he does have a reason to finger an innocent person, or at least not to finger the real guilty party because he may be his friend or he may be afraid of him. Some other evidence must link the second person to the crime. Otherwise, it would be easy for the first person to simply name anybody in order to get a lighter sentence."

The judge lifted a square of fried tofu with his chopsticks and continued. "Let's say I never saw the face of the person who robbed me, but when he turned and ran, I, or some other witness to the crime, saw that he had green hair. Our Mr. Smith has green hair. 'Green hair' might be sufficient corroborating evidence.

"In other courts where you do not need corroboration as a matter of law, the jury is told to scrutinize the credibility of the cooperating witness with great care."

Back to the courtroom and the corroborating evidence against Joe Chen.

THE CORROBORATORS

Leemie's first corroborating evidence comes from Detective David Chan. He conducted the lineups for the two victims, Mr. Wang and Mr. Li.

Dave describes what transpired during the lineups. Leemie reminds the jury that the first victim knew Jane Ding and Sonny Chen and could easily identify them. He also saw Cow Eyes. The second victim knew Johnny Ding by his nickname, Charlie Chan, and immediately picked him out. Arresting and convicting these three were relatively easy. Joe Chen is another matter. Neither victim ever saw his face.

> **THE DETECTIVE EXPLAINS LINEUPS:**
>
> A lineup is an identification procedure. We place a suspect in a lineup with five other individuals who are about the same age, race, and features as the suspect.
>
> There are usually six people, including the suspect, in the lineup. The suspect can stand anywhere he or she chooses.

The detective describes Joe Chen's arrest and then helps Leemie lay the foundation for the second corroborating witness, a Bell Telephone investigator, by reporting various steps in the investigation.

Although Mr. Wang and Mr. Li were unable to tell the detectives where they were being held, they did have a phone number for the apartment. Apparently Mr. Li's father refused to pay any money until he knew that his son was alive. He told the kidnappers, "I want to be able to call him." The kidnappers then gave the father their telephone number at the Rivington Street apartment.

During the investigation, Mr. Li's parents, in China, searched through their bills and found the phone number. Later, Leemie says, "The group had accomplices in China, but we have no idea who they are." The detectives submitted that phone number to the D.A.'s office. They, in turn, subpoenaed Bell Telephone for subscriber information. From there they were able to get the address of the apartment. The detectives went to that location and learned that it was rented to Joe Chen. Leemie believes that this is part of the evidence that supports the testimony of her cooperating witnesses.

Glenn disagrees. He does not think that this is corroborating evidence. Remember, everyone already admits that the apartment is rented in Joe Chen's name and the telephone is listed in Joe Chen's name. For Glenn, the telephone investigator's testimony adds nothing. When the defense attorney cross-examines the detective, he once again stresses the fact that his client wasn't described as the leader of the kidnappers until after Johnny Ding was arrested. "And up until the time of that arrest," Glenn asks the detective, "there was no information provided to you that Joe Chen was ever involved in this kidnapping, isn't that correct?"

"Correct," says Dave. He leans back in his chair, totally relaxed.

Glenn tries to work the detective's responses to his advantage. He points out differences between the witnesses' descriptions on the witness stand and their descriptions recorded during the interrogations. Take, for example, the sunglasses.

Glenn later says, "If I remember correctly, the sunglasses belonged to Cow Eyes. He is a big, lanky guy—a bad dude. Jane Ding described him as the guy with the sunglasses. At one point, I think it was the second complainant who said that the leader was wearing sunglasses. *'The dailo had sunglasses.'* I was trying to show that that person was Cow Eyes, who played a leadership role until Johnny Ding arrived on the scene, and that Johnny Ding was actually the true leader."

Another inconsistency: the physical descriptions of the kidnappers. The second victim said that Johnny Ding is six feet tall. But, in fact, he is only five five. The tallest member of the group is Cow Eyes, who is five eleven. Again, this supports Glenn's theory that Cow Eyes was a leader.

But later, away from the jury, the detective gives a different explanation about why there are mistaken identifications in criminal investigations. "Here's a person who just went through the worst experience of his whole life. He was blindfolded and beaten and tortured, the whole bit. Put yourself in his shoes. Could you remember the heights and the names and characteristics of every one of these people? Would you be able to explain it all to a detective over the telephone? Would it come out totally accurate? That's very, very hard."

Hard or easy, in Glenn's view this corroborating evidence will not hurt his client. After all, no one, other than witnesses who have much to gain, has implicated Joe Chen as a kidnapper, much less the dailo. If Glenn can produce a strong defense, he just might be able to win a not-guilty verdict for his client.

Then Leemie calls a new witness.

ECHO

Once Detective Chan steps down, the jury takes a break and Leemie prepares to call her next witness to the stand. Glenn is not happy about this turn of events. "What's the nature of this testimony?" he asks. "I was told about this witness at ten o'clock this morning. After the direct examination, I ask that we break for lunch so that I have an opportunity to consider her testimony and that—"

JUDGE FRIED SAYS:
In a criminal case the defendant is entitled to know who the witnesses are so that his lawyer can prepare an effective cross-examination.

"Offer of proof" is advance information about what the witness is going to talk about.

"We will break for lunch after direct—if it's finished. If it is not finished, we'll finish it after lunch," Judge Fried replies.

Glenn will not back down. "First of all, I ask for an offer of proof about what this witness is going to say. This witness is not on the witness list."

All along it had been Glenn's understanding that every one of the witnesses who could connect Joe Chen to the kidnappings had cooperation agreements as indicted codefendants. He based his defense on the fact that these witnesses are not credible. Now a new witness, who did not participate in the kidnapping, may place Joe Chen at the crime. Glenn demands an answer. "I need to know the nature of this testimony."

"Let me hear in a sentence what the offer of proof is," Judge Fried asks Leemie.

Leemie explains that the new witness visited the apartment during the time of the kidnapping and that on one occasion she heard the defendant give an order for the victims to be beaten.

"There's your offer of proof." The judge looks down at Glenn. "What is the issue with the witness?"

"The issue is, Your Honor, that this is the first time that I'm finding out about it," his voice strains. "It is distinct from every representation the prosecutor has made about what proof would occur in this case." Glenn is so angry he can barely look at Leemie.

"How can I keep her from calling this witness? What basis could there be for me to do that?" Judge Fried asks Glenn.

The basis is the fact that this witness is a surprise. Glenn wants time to research any legal arguments about producing her at the last minute. Glenn's body stiffens. "The witness is not on the witness list," he repeats.

When asked why the witness is not on the list, Leemie respectfully explains that after her interview with Echo, she didn't think that the woman would ever show up at the trial. Months before the trial Leemie had interviewed Echo along with other possible witnesses. After their interview, Leemie decided not to call her. But once Johnny Ding testified, the prosecutor changed her mind because she thought that Echo could help make Johnny seem more sympathetic.

Last Friday her detectives combed the sweatshops in Chinatown searching for Echo. They found her and told her to come to court Monday. To everyone's surprise, Echo showed up. Now it is up to the judge to decide whether or not Echo may testify, even though she is not on the witness list. The courtroom is silent.

Three seconds pass.

Five seconds.

Ten.

"Call your next witness."

Judge Fried looks at the defense attorney, who is slumped in his chair. After Leemie's direct examination the judge will give Glenn extra time to prepare for his cross.

"At this time the People call Miss Echo," Leemie announces after the jurors have taken their seats.

Like the two cooperating witnesses, Echo does not look at Joe Chen when she enters the courtroom. Dressed in a red-and-white check shirt, overalls, and black cotton jacket, twenty-three-year-old Echo is not as ordinary looking as Jane Ding, nor as glamorous as the defendant's girlfriend. She tells the jury that she is a graduate of elementary school and speaks both Mandarin and Fujianese. She came to America in June 1994, after a three-month boat ride for which her family paid the snake head $25,000. Two days after her release, she started working in a sweatshop. "I sew clothes from nine A.M. to ten at night, six days a week." She still has to repay $10,000 of her smuggling debt. She sends money to her mother in China every month.

Six months after Johnny Ding arrived in America, he met Echo. They have been going together ever since. When Johnny moved to Baltimore, though, she remained in New York, unwilling to give up her steady paycheck working in the garment factory. Then, when Johnny returned (with the second victim), he called her. She spent a number of nights in the apartment where the kidnapped victims were being held. The second victim, Mr. Li, said that one woman was kind to him while he was held. She gave him food and talked to him. That woman was Echo.

LUNCH BREAK

Once the jury leaves the courtroom, Glenn asks if Echo is under arrest. She is not. Glenn wants to talk with the witness.

But he knows that an interview with Echo will be difficult. She has just been escorted out into the hallway behind the courtroom. Glenn believes that there are a number of detectives back there with her. "Will she talk to me freely with the detectives watching us?"

Judge Fried asks Leemie to see if Echo would be willing to speak with the defense attorney. Glenn

> **JUDGE FRIED SAYS:**
> A witness can be subpoenaed to testify in a courtroom, but cannot be forced to talk to the other side.

wants to be present when Leemie asks Echo; he does not trust the prosecution. But Judge Fried says that she can make this inquiry alone.

Leemie returns with the announcement that Echo does not want to talk to the defense attorney. "She is in a state of confusion and is afraid and upset because she didn't know that she was going to be testifying today," Leemie explains. "I volunteered that I would be present during Glenn's talk with her, but she is in a very agitated state right now."

Once again anger bubbles from deep inside the defender. He protests that the prosecutor was outside for only four minutes. He complains that detectives are in the hall with the witness. Later Glenn recalls why he wanted to be present when Leemie spoke with Echo. "Once I heard that Leemie was allowed to speak with Echo alone, I knew it was all over. It is not uncommon for lawyers—on both sides—to tell their witness in a persuasive way why it is not in their best interest to speak to opposing counsel. Ninety-nine out of a hundred times a witness will elect not to speak to an opposing attorney. And that's what I think happened here."

"There are no police officers," Leemie says. "She is standing in the back hallway with a Mandarin interpreter, who is female." Leemie is determined not to let Glenn's emotional outbursts get her off track. The two victims are counting on her. No one—not even a nice guy like Glenn—will come between these victims and her evidence.

But Joe Chen is counting on Glenn. And no one—not even nice guys like the two victims—will interfere with Glenn's client's right to a fair trial.

· · ·

When court is adjourned for lunch, Glenn races two blocks back to his office. "Damn!" he yells, throwing

> **DISCRETIONARY RULINGS:**
> In certain specific instances a judge may rule according to the dictates of his or her own conscience and judgment, within the bounds of the principles of law.

his briefcase on the floor. "Can I block this witness?" He cannot. The judge has the discretionary right to make this ruling.

Glenn calls two defense lawyers, friends, who have had a great deal of trial experience. They hurry over to help plan strategy for Glenn's cross-examination. "Treat her gently but firmly," they advise, "and get her off the stand as soon as possible." The lawyers decide that the cross-examination should focus on two issues: Echo's immigration status and her relationship with her boyfriend, Johnny Ding.

AFTERNOON SESSION

After the lunch break Leemie has Echo describe some of the same events that were mentioned earlier in the trial. She talks about the time the second victim told her he was kidnapped by Johnny Ding. Three jurors nod in recognition of the incident—a point not missed by the two lawyers.

Later, Leemie explained why she asked these questions. "You always try to reinforce what the complaining witnesses said earlier in the trial."

CROSS-EXAMINATION

"Are you aware that you could be deported?" Glenn asks, implying that the government has pressured Echo into testifying.

In barely a whisper Echo admits that deportation is a concern. Glenn raises one eyebrow and moves on to another point.

A second reason for Echo to lie is the "stand by your man" motive. When Echo admits that she knows that Johnny Ding is cooperating with the government in order to get a lighter sentence, Glenn glances over at the jury again. Convinced that the jury got both his points, Glenn quickly ends his cross.

REDIRECT

Leemie moves in for damage control. "Did anyone threaten you to get you to come to court today?"

"Objection!" shouts Glenn. He believes that Leemie's question has nothing to do with his cross-examination.

"She can ask that," the judge says.

Glenn asks to approach the bench.

"Sure," agrees the judge pleasantly.

Once at the side, Glenn complains that Leemie is giving an improper line of redirect. "My cross was designed to show that she may have been frightened and *concerned* about the government, not that she has been *threatened* by them. And I made a *specific* effort not to suggest that she had been threatened." Here is another instance where paying attention to words and their implications is especially important.

Leemie is fast. "Judge, I think that the fact that he even raised the issue—that she is *concerned* about deportation—leaves open the question whether or not she was threatened."

Leemie's next move, Glenn declares, will surely be to ask Echo if promises were made (on Johnny Ding's behalf) in return for her testimony. There is no reason she cannot ask that question, especially since Glenn brought up the "stand by your man" notion during his cross-examination.

Back in open court Leemie does exactly as Glenn had anticipated. "Did anyone make you a promise for your testimony today?" she asks Echo.

"No."

"Same objection, Your Honor."

"Objection overruled."

"Were there any promises made to you that have to do with your boyfriend or his sentence in order to get you to come and testify today?"

"Same objection," says the defense attorney. Glenn wants his objections on record in case Joe Chen is found guilty and asks for an appeal.

"Same ruling, it is overruled."

"No," answers the witness. Leemie is convinced that she successfully eliminated any suspicion that the government would either threaten or make promises to Echo for her testimony. "I have no further questions."

Glenn, who is still satisfied that the jury will agree with him that Echo is not a credible witness, has no further questions either.

· · ·

REMINDER:
The defense does not have to produce witnesses. The defense only has to undermine the prosecutor's case.

A MOTION:
This is a formal request, or petition, made by a lawyer to test the constitutionality of the manner in which a statement, physical evidence, or an identification procedure (such as photographs or a lineup) has been obtained.

Lawyers also make an "application for a motion" to challenge the admissibility of evidence. If the judge grants the motion, the evidence cannot be used.

"That's it for this afternoon, ladies and gentlemen," the judge tells the jury. "There are some legal issues I must deal with. We are going to resume tomorrow morning in this courtroom at ten o'clock. Please do not discuss the case amongst yourselves. Have a good evening."

The trial is moving faster than anyone thought. The end of the prosecutor's case is minutes away. Judge Fried asks Glenn if there will be witnesses for the defense. Glenn reports that he is planning to call witnesses.

After the prosecutor rests, the defense will make his motion to dismiss the case. If Judge Fried denies the motion, the defense must be ready. Glenn returns to his office to prepare the motion, even though he knows that the chances that this will be granted are one in a million.

· · ·

Judge Fried sprints downstairs to his chambers and asks his law clerk, Elizabeth, to begin preparing the charge to the jury for when it is needed.

Elizabeth searches the file cabinet for a previous similar case to use as the framework for the charges.

"Did you find it?" the judge asks her while taking off his robe.

"No."

"Watch this!" he says with a flourish. The judge reaches into the files, expecting to come up with it fast. Not there. Elizabeth giggles. He rummages through the cabinet while Elizabeth works at her desk, trying hard not to laugh. "I see that smirk," he says merrily. "I'll find it yet." He digs deeper. Elizabeth's head is partially hidden behind stacks of legal paper that sit on her desk. Mrs. Cassidy telephones to say that the judge is needed in the courtroom for a pretrial hearing on a different case.

"You'll see." He turns to Elizabeth lightheartedly. "It'll come to me when I'm on the bench."

"Yeah, yeah," she laughs.

TIME: LATER THAT EVENING
PLACE: GLENN'S OFFICE

Glenn returns to his office for his late-night meeting with a mystery witness. While waiting, he pores over tons of case law to help him build an argument for yet another continuance to prepare his case. The judge will deny it, of course, because he doesn't want to hold the jury any longer than absolutely necessary. But Glenn works on a brief anyway. If Joe Chen is convicted, the themes in this motion could later set the bases for an appeal.

Just before the mystery witness is due to arrive, Glenn asks everyone to leave the offices. In general, defense lawyers tend toward a heightened state of distrust when the government is involved. Glenn is particularly apprehensive about the state finding this witness before he has a chance to talk to him. He even pulls down his blinds.

A tall, skinny man enters the darkened waiting room.

THE PEOPLE REST

- LEEMIE READS JOE CHEN'S STATEMENT.
- LEEMIE COMPLETES THE PEOPLE'S CASE AGAINST JOE CHEN.
- GLENN REVEALS THE NAMES OF THE WITNESSES FOR THE DEFENSE.
- WILL JOE CHEN TESTIFY?

TIME: TUESDAY, APRIL 28, 1998; 9:35 A.M.
PLACE: JUDGE FRIED'S COURTROOM

Glenn sits in the empty jury box reviewing his notes. Last night he worked late, interviewing his mystery witness. Because this man does not speak English, a court-appointed interpreter worked with them. Feeling sorry for the interpreter, who worked so long and so hard, Glenn invited him out to dinner. At ten-thirty P.M., just after they left the office, Glenn's wife called. When there was no answer, and he didn't return home, she became worried. "She thought I'd been kidnapped," Glenn says, chuckling.

Leemie arrives, pushing a cart that is piled high with files that relate to the case. She places a few folders on the prosecutor's table and sits down to write. The lawyers no longer say good morning to each other. Guards escort Joe Chen to the defense table, Glenn joins him, the judge arrives, and the members of the jury enter and take their assigned seats.

Leemie says, "At this time the People call Detective Robert Sassok, Shield #3031, Major Case Squad, Asian Crime Team." The detective is on the witness stand to testify about when Joe Chen gave Leemie and other law enforcement officials a statement about the kidnappings. It was Detective Sassok who escorted Joe Chen from pretrial detention to Leemie's office in the district attorney's building. Leemie's supervisor, Carla Freedman, and a translator were also present at this meeting. They sat in a circle, with Joe Chen handcuffed to his chair. After Leemie read Joe Chen his Miranda rights, he answered questions and talked about his knowledge of the kidnappings. This is the second time Joe Chen talked to law officials about the kidnapping. His first statement—which had been an issue at a pretrial hearing and will be described later in this book—cannot be read to the jury.

Leemie reads the second statement to the jury.

JOE CHEN'S STATEMENT
TIME: JULY 2, 1997; 6:50 P.M.
PLACE: THE DISTRICT ATTORNEY'S OFFICE

I lived in a basement apartment on Rivington Street. Luke Chen [Cow Eyes], Sonny Chen, and Jane Ding had a conversation concerning a man who was smuggled into the country. He had money. Jane Ding was told to bring the man back to the apartment. The man was brought to the apartment. I only saw his back. I was in the room in the back when he was brought in. I saw they pushed him inside a room when the man was brought into the apartment.

After the man was in the apartment, I was in the apartment for a half an hour. Four days later I came back because I rented the place. In the apartment was my brother, Luke, Jane, and Johnny Ding's girlfriend. I did not see the man. I was talking to them about the apartment because the apartment and phone were in my name. I saw them talking about how to get the money from the man's family in China. At the time I saw Johnny Ding bring another man out to use the rest room. It was not the same man from four days ago. Johnny Ding brought the second man from the same room that the first man was put in. The second man was blindfolded with a piece of cloth. He was not handcuffed. I did not know what they were doing at the time. My concern was the apartment. I was in the apartment a half an hour.

Three days later my brother called. They moved things out of the apartment: pots, pans, things like that. Later I learned they moved to Eldridge Street. My brother said he had kidnapped two people, taking their money, and let the two people go.

I went to the landlord. I still had one month deposit. I could not find the landlord so I gave up. I had moved out everything. I did not go back to the apartment.

I spoke to my brother two or three months later. He said nothing about the man in the apartment. Luke said nothing. We were both busy.

Johnny Ding, I saw in the street. I had met Johnny Ding two or three times before this. We are from the same village. We went to a restaurant, and we had a drink. We got drunk and we had karaoke. I wanted to sing and he wanted to sing, and we had an argument. I have not spoken to him since. I passed him on the street, we did not speak.

My brother is in jail. Sometimes I talk to him, sometimes I send him money. Jane Ding is in jail. No one lived in Rivington Street after I got moved out.

Not present when the two men were let go. I am not sure if my brother was there, but he said they were let go.

I read in newspaper, and I was told, that Johnny Ding is in jail. People are talking about it. I was not lying. I am telling the truth. Between us, Johnny Ding and me have—we have bad blood, and he will accuse me.

I didn't do this. What can I say? Why did they say this? Well, they accused me of something I did not do. I did not lie to you. This thing has nothing to do with me. I only saw them. I had already moved out.

When the detective asked Joe Chen why he did not call the police, he said, "He's my brother. If I called the police, he would be in trouble. I was scared because the apartment and phone was under my name."

The detective asked him where he worked. Joe Chen said that he worked with his cousin, but he never described the kind of work he did. He did, however, add that his girlfriend worked in a barbershop. "She works all day and comes home at eleven P.M., except for her day off."

"I know you paid people for this kidnapping," Detective Sassok says to Joe Chen.

"This is impossible."

"I know you paid Johnny Ding for bringing the man from Baltimore."

"Nonsense. It is a false accusation."

"Did you owe money to the people?" the detective asked, referring to his original smuggling fee.

"I owe money to the snake heads. My brother owes money. My

cousin also owes money. I am telling the truth, but I do not know if you will believe me. This case has nothing to do with me. What difference does it make?"

Joe Chen's statement goes on to detail what went on in the apartment: the phone calls to China, the yelling, the screaming, the beatings. "Johnny Ding was demanding $8,000 from the second man. I know they did collect. This is common sense; otherwise, why did they let them go? Johnny Ding, not my brother, planned it. They shared the money, Johnny Ding and my brother."

End of statement read by Detective Sassok.
21:20 hours [9:20 P.M.], July 2, 1997.
Signed by the detective and the defendant.

The time has come for Leemie to question her last witness, an investigator for Bell Atlantic. He confirms that calls were made from a telephone assigned to Joe Chen to the victims' families in China. During the cross-examination, Glenn demonstrates that there is no way of knowing who actually made the calls or who actually paid the phone bill. But as far as Leemie is concerned, the telephone records, Joe Chen's statement, and Echo's eyewitness account add up to plenty of corroborating evidence to convict Joe Chen. She says that she is particularly happy with Echo's testimony because she is not an informant and was able to positively identify the defendant.

Judge Fried asks the prosecutor, "Do the People have anything further?"

"Nothing."

"The People rest at this point?"

One would expect that "the People rest" is a dramatic moment in the trial. Not at all. Leemie simply replies, "Yes, judge."

Judge Fried says to the jurors. "We are going to need some time, ladies and gentlemen. The People have rested. That completes the presentation of their case."

.　　.　　.

"I didn't feel anything as much as tired," Leemie says after the trial. "It's not a great sense of relief because I still have the summation, which is really, really hard to prepare. Logistically my part is over, but at the same time, I want to keep my adrenaline going until I get a verdict."

Leemie will not live a normal life until the verdict is in. She continues to spend her nights reading the trial's transcripts, reviewing notes, and, most important, working on her summation. "Basically, when you are on trial, you are totally obsessed and absorbed," she explains. "Your whole life is the trial. You go to sleep thinking about the trial and you wake up thinking about the trial."

In the remaining days some lawyers from the district attorney's office and support staff from the Asian Gang Squad drop by the courtroom to watch the proceedings. The two detectives, Dave Chan and Hayman Goon, linger in the back hall. Because they can still be re-called as witnesses, they cannot watch the proceedings. "What happened in there? What's going on?" they ask when observers leave the courtroom.

Mr. Wang, the first victim, frequently telephones both Leemie and the detectives to learn how the trial is proceeding. Mr. Li, the second victim, does not call. He wants nothing more to do with the incident he described as an "experience I will always remember."

As expected, Glenn petitions the court to dismiss the case. And as expected, the judge denies the motion. But there are still issues to take care of before the defense opens its case, especially if Joe Chen chooses to testify on his own behalf.

SANDOVAL RULE

Glenn says, "As Joe Chen's legal strategist, I can advise him against testifying, but I can't stop him. If he tells me, 'I want to testify, I gotta tell my story,' I must have the Sandoval ruling in place as advance protection."

Glenn knows that his client has been accused of other crimes that will make him look bad to the jury. He wants to be sure that they don't come out. If they did, and he is asked about them, Joe Chen would have to plead the Fifth Amendment. "These are open cases that my client could eventually be charged with," Glenn later explains. "I took the position that any uncharged crimes should not be used during Leemie's cross-examination. If he did not plead the Fifth, he would be opening himself up to more prosecution."

. . .

Leemie asks about Glenn's witness list. The defense lawyer will first call Detective Hayman Goon to the stand.

"For what purpose?" asks the prosecutor coldly.

"Am I required to disclose that?" Glenn looks up at the judge.

"I think you should give a general statement," Judge Fried replies.

"He was involved in the arrest from the beginning. He is actually the police officer from the Major Case Squad who has had more involvement in the investigation than anybody else. There are some questions that I need to ask about

> **SANDOVAL RULE:**
> Generally, if a defendant chooses to testify, he is entitled to an advance ruling about what prior bad acts, or prior crimes, the prosecution will be able to pursue during cross-examination.
>
> This rule applies only to the defendant, not to witnesses.

> **THE FIFTH AMENDMENT TO THE U.S. CONSTITUTION:**
> "No person shall be held to answer for a capital, or otherwise infamous crime, unless on a presentment or indictment of a grand jury, except in cases arising in the land or naval forces, or in the militia, when in actual service in time of war or public danger; nor shall any person be subject for the same offense to be twice put in jeopardy of life or limb; nor shall he be compelled in any criminal case to be a witness against himself, nor be deprived of life, liberty, or property, without due process of law; nor shall private property be taken for public use, without just compensation."

his initial dealings with the complainants and other aspects of the investigation."

Judge Fried agrees that he is an appropriate witness. "Who else do you have?"

"At this point, Your Honor, there is a witness—I don't want to disclose the name yet because I have to meet with him again over the lunch break."

"And what is the offer of proof?" Leemie charges.

Glenn will not disclose that either, not until the witness takes the stand. Unlike the prosecutor, the defense need not reveal testimony ahead of time. Because the defense does not have the many resources of the state, there is no worry that it will abuse its powers.

"Next," says Judge Fried quickly. He does not want more bickering.

Suzy Ling is the defendant's girlfriend. She will be a witness for the defense. "I believe Ms. Kahng already has her date of birth, her rap sheet, and as much information as she needs about her."

If Suzy Ling testifies, Leemie wants to ask her questions about a time when Joe Chen assaulted her. When Suzy reported the incident to the police, Joe Chen was arrested. But because of their relationship, she would not testify against him in court, and the case was dropped. Clearly Glenn does not want the jury to know that Joe Chen beat up his girlfriend. The lawyers argue yet again. Leemie stands ramrod straight, facing the judge, while Glenn paces back and forth.

They debate. They contest. Their arguments seem to go on forever. The judge has heard enough. He leans forward, glaring down at the lawyers. It's a look that stops everyone dead. The judge sits back and says, "If Ms. Ling testifies, I will permit the assistant [Leemie] to ask if Joe Chen hit Ms. Ling. I will permit this simple question: 'In April of 1997, did you file a complaint against the defendant with the police, and then drop that complaint and not appear?' If the answer to that question is yes, that will end it. If she answers no, then before you ask her any further questions, come to the side."

"Okay," says Leemie.

The judge looks to the glum defense attorney. "If this question is asked, do you want me to give an instruction to the jury that this particular testimony is not to be considered as relevant to the guilt or nonguilt of the defendant, but simply to the credibility of the witness?"

"Yes," says Glenn, "but not until the end of the testimony." He doesn't want this damning testimony to be dramatized any more than it already will be.

Next.

Even before the trial began, Glenn talked with Joe about his right to testify on his own behalf. Joe did not want to testify. Now that the prosecutor's case is revealed, Glenn asks for time to revisit Joe's decision.

The lawyer and the defendant huddle at the defense table. This is Joe's last chance to decide whether or not to testify. If he testifies, he opens himself up to Leemie's questions about other crimes, such as his assault on his girlfriend. If he does not testify, the jury won't hear his account of the kidnapping.

· · ·

The courtroom becomes eerily quiet. Only soft whispers from the defense table and the sound of pages turning break the stillness. Leemie reviews her notes. Judge Fried thumbs through the latest issue of *The New York Law Journal.* Every once in a while he looks up to see if Glenn is ready.

Glenn, Joe, and his interpreter continue whispering. The jury waits in the hallway. The guards shuffle their feet.

Finally Glenn signals the judge that they are ready. Joe Chen has reached a decision.

No, he will not testify.

.   .   .

At the end of the day Joe Chen prepares to be escorted back to his cell. He knows the routine well. Passively he places his hands behind his back for the guards to handcuff him. Glenn pats his shoulder affectionately and tucks a yellow legal pad under his arm. On the pad are the many issues that could come up if Joe Chen decided to testify.

Returning to the cluttered defense table, Glenn begins packing his briefcase. He looks at Joe's now empty chair and says to no one in particular, "It's tough being a defense lawyer."

THE FRUIT OF THE POISONOUS TREE

- THE DEFENSE BEGINS ITS CASE.
- WHAT HAPPENED AFTER JOE CHEN WAS ARRESTED.
- JOE CHEN GIVES TWO STATEMENTS TO LAW ENFORCEMENT.
- JOE CHEN'S GIRLFRIEND HIRES GLENN AS DEFENSE ATTORNEY.
- GLENN GOES BEFORE THE JUDGE IN A PRETRIAL HEARING TO SUPPRESS HIS CLIENT'S STATEMENTS.

TIME: MONDAY, APRIL 27, 1998; AFTER COURT
PLACE: GLENN GARBER'S LAW OFFICE

It's the last night before the defense of Joe Chen begins. Glenn still has a potential witness to interview and some last-minute strategies to work out. Oddly, he does not seem anxious. He says that he is doing a job that he loves. When asked why, he smiles.

I always was for the little man. I felt bad for the kids being picked on. Even in high school I championed the little guy's rights. That often put me in conflict with my teachers. If I thought they were treating somebody improperly, I would speak up. I was probably totally obnoxious.

Once I got into criminal defense work, it got into my blood. I start from the standpoint that my client is innocent. My approach is that the gov-

ernment is doing something wrong to my client. I fight from that position. That's what keeps me going.

I grew up in an affluent, suburban community in northern New Jersey. My parents' parents were immigrants who came here from Poland and Austria. They are good, honest people. My dad worked his way up from nothing to become a doctor. Mom's a homemaker. My parents are very liberal and very supportive.

I went to Syracuse University and then Cardozo Law School. My wife is a lawyer too, but she is not practicing right now. We met when we both worked as summer associates in a big firm in New Jersey.

PUBLIC DEFENDER:
A lawyer paid by the state to represent a criminal defendant who cannot afford an attorney.

For three and a half years I was a public defender for the Legal Aid Society, representing indigent defendants in New York City. I got a lot of trial experience there.

My law partner was also a Legal Aid attorney. At first we had very little money. Our office wasn't really an office. It was a mail drop and a phone service. We literally worked out of our briefcases. We held meetings in other people's offices during their lunch breaks. I don't think I made more than a couple hundred dollars in a six-month period.

Just after I left Legal Aid, I had one of my most serious cases: an Asian kidnapping case. Actually, it was in front of Judge Fried, but I'm sure he doesn't remember it.

There were five defendants in the case and I did a pretty good job for my guy. As I remember it, there was a hearing where the judge ordered the witnesses to come in and testify. But they never came forward, so the case was dismissed. That defendant thought I was the greatest thing on earth. He apparently was a big honcho in an Asian gang. He kept referring a lot of cases to me.

Once the cases started coming, things kicked into gear. We rented a *real office, which was basically a hole in the wall. After about four and a half years we did well enough to move here. This place is beautiful.*

One kidnapping case I handled was a six-week trial in Queens. There were many defendants in that one, too, and everyone was acquitted. My client was facing fifty to life, just like Joe Chen is now. We won.

I like representing indigent people. I always did. For rich defendants, I see the balance shifts a little bit. Clients with money, and who are better educated, don't do stupid things like make statements to the police. They don't have terrible prior records that slap them in the face. They have a level of sophistication that doesn't exist with most indigent clients.

My biggest concern is that I don't lose my idealism.

The preparation for Joe's defense began long before the trial began. The first very important skirmish took place soon after Joe was arrested, when he made two statements to law enforcement. The second statement was the one Leemie read to the jury at the close of the People's case. The first one was not admissible in court. Here's what happened:

THE INTERROGATION—FIRST STATEMENT

Joe Chen was arrested and taken to an interrogation room, where he was searched and cuffed to a chair. Because he spoke only a little English, the detective called an interpreter to translate the Miranda warning. No questions could be asked until the interpreter arrived. Detective David Chan asked Joe if he would like a glass of water, and then he left him alone until they were able to talk.

At two-fifteen P.M. the interpreter arrived and the detective read Joe his Miranda rights. After each question on the Miranda list, the defendant answered yes and signed his name.

Then Joe gave the detective his statement. Afterward the detective read it back to him and asked if he wanted to change anything. No changes were necessary.

At three-thirty P.M. Joe Chen was taken to another room and handcuffed to another chair while the detective began the paperwork needed for the arrest processing. Both Joe and the interpreter were given food while they waited. The detective called Leemie and described the substance of Joe's statement. What happened during the next three hours became the first of many disputes between Leemie and Glenn.

THE INTERROGATION—SECOND STATEMENT

By six-thirty P.M. another detective from the Major Case Squad, Robert Sassok, took Joe from the jailhouse to a room near Leemie's office. Later, the judge commented in one of his rulings that this "may be inaccurate since there is no record in the Central Booking [prison] log book that the defendant was received by the Department of Correction."

At seven P.M. Leemie met Joe for the first time. She says, "In very serious cases it is a good idea to talk to the defendant. We can get a sense of where the case is going—is he inclined to talk, is he inclined not to talk, and so forth."

Leemie read him his Miranda rights again before she asked questions. Joe drank a soda, smoked a cigarette, and made a second statement, the one that was read to the jury.

Up to this point Joe had been talking to Leemie and the detectives without benefit of a lawyer.

DATE: JULY 5, 1997
PLACE: GLENN GARBER'S OFFICE

Suzy Ling hired Glenn to represent her boyfriend, Joe. Glenn already knew the defendant because he had represented him once before in a robbery case. In that case the charge against Joe was dismissed. After describing the situation, Suzy paid Glenn a fee to retain his services. This is all the money she had from her work at a local massage parlor.

When Glenn met with Joe, he insisted that he was innocent, that he never kidnapped those two men. The first thing Glenn tried to do was have the bail reduced. But this is an A-1 felony, the most serious type of crime—no bail.

The case was brought before the grand jury. The jurors listened to Leemie's evidence and returned an indictment against Joe.

Leemie then offered a deal: If Joe Chen pleaded guilty, he would be given the same sentence as his family members. No deal. Joe Chen wanted his day in court. Leemie says, "I offered the plea right up until the jury was chosen. That would spare the victims from having to come forward, and it would spare us from burning informants. ["Burning informants" means having cooperating witnesses come forward and testify in open court, thus revealing that they are informants.] I don't know why he decided to go to trial. I don't know if he is stubborn, if he is stoic. Perhaps he was waiting to see if people would come forward.

"Glenn is not the kind of lawyer who browbeats his client to take a plea," Leemie says. "If Joe Chen wanted a trial—and he's entitled to a trial—Glenn would do the trial."

> **GRAND JURY:**
> In New York and many other states the grand jury's job is to determine if there is enough evidence to indict a defendant. An indictment is an accusation by a grand jury of a public offense that is punishable by law.
>
> The grand jury does not determine guilt or nonguilt.

· · ·

Glenn's first line of defense was to try to overturn the evidence against his client. He worked on a number of motions that he would bring before Judge Fried in a series of pretrial sessions. The most important motion had to do with the two statements Joe Chen made after he was arrested. If Joe Chen's statements were taken illegally, they could not be used in court.

In Glenn's view, Joe Chen was improperly arrested at his home without a warrant. "You can't do that," he says. "That would be considered an invasion of privacy. Police officers must first contact a judge and say, 'Look, judge, we have probable cause that this guy committed a crime. Give us an arrest warrant so we can invade his home and arrest him.'" Then they must tell the judge the basis for the probable cause. Glenn wanted the two statements Joe gave to the prosecution thrown out because they were made during an illegal arrest.

Leemie disagreed. "It was not an illegal arrest because Joe Chen was not at his *own* home but visiting his girlfriend's apartment." There was no improper invasion of his privacy. Which claim was true?

REMINDER

Seeking the truth is not the only purpose of a trial. The most important other purpose is to keep the government, with its immense power, from overreaching. Even if it appears obvious that a defendant has committed a terrible crime, guilt can be proved only through legitimate methods. If evidence has not been legally obtained, the prosecutor cannot use it. The defendant may go free, even though, in truth, he or she is guilty. This threat keeps the government honest.

DATE: FEBRUARY 11. 1998
PLACE: JUDGE FRIED'S COURTROOM

Judge Fried cut to the chase. "There was an arrest of the defendant in an apartment. Thereafter statement number one and statement number two were made." Both lawyers nodded. So far so good.

Leemie had to be very careful. Joe Chen's statements were important pieces of evidence. The tiniest of technical mistakes could have nullified the arrest and set Joe Chen free. She argued that the detectives were given information by an informant to go to a certain apartment where they could find Joe, but they were not told that the defendant actually lived there. She added that after his arrest, Joe Chen himself said that he was at his girlfriend's apartment.

At the pretrial hearing, Glenn called the defendant's girlfriend to the witness stand. She told the court that at the time of his arrest, Joe Chen had been living with her, in her apartment, for nearly a year. All of his personal belongings were in the apartment. Therefore, in Glenn's view, it was Joe's home.

Suzy Ling was an effective witness. Glenn looked forward to her testimony in front of a jury.

ATTENUATION

Assuming Glenn was ruled correct, that Joe Chen's arrest was illegal, Leemie had another avenue to pursue. Leemie says, "I wasn't sure what would happen with the first statement, but I thought that under the law, the second statement was in my favor because of attenuation.

"I wanted to establish the fact that the second statement was not tainted by the first statement. There was a long time span between the two statements. They were given in different places. Different people were present. There was even a different interpreter. All these factors lead toward attenuation."

Glenn focused on Leemie's claim that Joe Chen was taken to different places between statements. "If

> **ATTENUATION:**
> If the defendant's statement is obtained after an illegal arrest, the statement is considered tainted, or in the words of the law, "the fruit of a poisonous tree."
>
> If substantial time has passed, and if different people do the questioning after giving the suspect new Miranda warnings, the new confession, or statement, may be cleansed of the taint, or "attenuated."

what she said was true, then the first stop would be the arraignment pen, called Central Booking. At the pretrial hearing, I called the arraignment captain to testify that my client had never made it to arraignment."

Soon after the last witness was excused, Judge Fried makes his ruling. "I find that the defendant had an expectation of privacy in his girlfriend's apartment, having lived there for one year, and that an arrest warrant was required before the police could have entered the apartment." Because of the warrantless arrest, Joe Chen's first statement was suppressed. It could not be used in a court of law before a jury. Glenn smiled broadly.

The second statement was a different matter. Seven hours had passed between the time of Joe Chen's arrest and his second statement. The circumstances had changed. The second statement was not tainted by the first. Attenuation had taken place and the second statement was admissible.

. . .

Still, Glenn is convinced that all Leemie's evidence is not enough to convict Joe Chen beyond a reasonable doubt.

HOSTILE WITNESS

- GLENN CALLS DETECTIVE HAYMAN GOON TO THE STAND.
- LEEMIE CROSS-EXAMINES THE DETECTIVE.

"Are you ready to call your next witness?" Judge Fried asks Glenn.

"Yes, I am." Glenn faces the jury. "The defense calls Detective Hayman Goon."

The detective is dressed in a gray business suit, white shirt, and red tie. He looks more like a lawyer than the lawyer, who by this time is totally drained. Detective Goon is part of the prosecutor's team and Glenn anticipates he will be difficult. Before asking a question, Glenn tells the jury that he has not talked to this witness in preparation for the trial. The detective is here under a court order.

Glenn asks permission to treat the detective as a hostile witness so that he can ask leading questions with yes and no answers.

"Why don't you start and we'll see where the testimony leads," the judge says.

According to Glenn, Hayman Goon is the backbone of the defense.

Glenn will use his testimony to show that there are differences between the witnesses' early descriptions and their courtroom testimony. These inconsistencies, Glenn believes, will raise reasonable doubt in the minds of the jurors.

First is the victims' belief that someone other than his client was the leader of the kidnappers. When Mr. Wang, the first victim, spoke with Detective Goon, he filled out a complaint report stating that a man called Johnny Ding was the leader of the kidnappers. "At no time did he tell you there was a person with a cell phone who was different from Johnny Ding?"

"Correct, sir." Detective Goon answers all the questions in crisp, military style: "Yes, sir," "No, sir."

Glenn puts the complaint report into evidence and moves on to the descriptions of the kidnappers. "Mr. Wang told you that Cow Eyes was five feet seven inches tall?" Glenn asks.

"I would have to refer to my notes, sir." The notes Hayman is talking about are the complaint report.

"You can actually hold it, if you want," Glenn says graciously.

"Thank you, sir." Some jurors snicker.

"You're welcome."

Hayman reads the notes to himself and replies that the report states that Cow Eyes is five seven. In fact, he is the tallest of the group, five eleven. Mr. Wang described Johnny Ding as five nine. He is really five five.

"There were differences in height amongst the perpetrators?"

"Oh, yes. Yes, sir." Hayman is smiling. He is certain that the jury won't care about this. Glenn smiles too. He is positive that the jury will see how important this is.

Glenn asks about notes that the detective took when he first questioned Jane Ding. In the notes Jane says that Johnny Ding is the leader of the kidnappers. She also talks about the kidnapping of Joe Chen's brother, Sonny.

Once again Leemie anticipates Glenn's next move. "Objection!" she calls. At the sidebar she tells the judge, "One, this is irrelevant. Two, he's trying to get Sonny Chen's kidnapping on the record without having to call Sonny Chen himself. Three, he's going to say Jane Ding has made prior inconsistent statements." Remember, Glenn is basing part of his defense on the fact that once, when Joe Chen's brother was kidnapped, he begged Johnny Ding to get the kidnappers to lower the ransom and he reported the crime to the police. If Joe Chen is such a sinister gangster, a dailo, no one would dare kidnap his brother. Glenn says, "It would be like kidnapping John Gotti's son." Besides, what kind of kidnapper calls the police to settle a dispute? He could take care of it on his own.

In any event, Leemie is right: Glenn does not want to call Joe Chen's brother as a witness. During Sonny's own interrogation he made a number of statements that were easily proved false. Glenn read the interrogation notes and knows that Leemie has enough ammunition to slaughter Sonny during cross-examination.

Judge Fried overrules Leemie's objection because Glenn is allowed to ask the detective about his notes. Glenn does exactly as Leemie anticipated. He asks if Jane Ding told the detective that Joe begged Johnny Ding for help in reducing his brother's kidnapping fee. Leemie jots down the word "begged" and underlines it.

Hayman answers, "Yes, sir," and Glenn moves on to another area that needs clearing up: Who is the real dailo? He wants to show that Johnny Ding is older than Joe Chen. Remember, the second victim said that the dailo, the leader, is always the oldest.

"Now, are you aware of the age of Joe Chen?" Glenn asks Hayman.

"No, sir."

Glenn is surprised by the response. He tries again. "Is it fair to say that he's twenty-six years old?"

"Objection!" The detective already said that he does not know the defendant's age.

"Sustained."

Glenn tries a third approach. "Is there anything that would refresh your memory about his age?"

"His online booking sheet, sir." Glenn is just about to hand the detective an online booking sheet when Leemie objects.

"Let's go to the side," Judge Fried says, rising. Once they are away from the jury, the judge asks, "Objection, Ms. Kahng?"

"This is not Detective Goon's online booking sheet," she replies. "Detective Goon did not participate in the arrest of Joe Chen. His partner arrested him." Leemie cannot afford to let one detail slip by.

Glenn is not concerned about such petty issues as who has whose booking sheet. But a trial is based on hundreds of small details, any one of which could make the difference between conviction and acquittal.

The lawyers argue again. Judge Fried stops the quibbling. "If he has personal knowledge of the age—"

Glenn cuts him midsentence. "He said that the online booking sheet would refresh his memory."

Leemie crosses her arms across her chest and clenches her fists. "But that's not his online booking sheet."

Judge Fried agrees with the prosecutor. Glenn may ask the detective only about his personal knowledge of the defendant's age.

> **JUDGE FRIED SAYS:**
> Throughout a trial the lawyers often become involved in issues that are tempests in a teapot. That's what is happening here. My job is to cut through this and keep the trial on track.

"Then I will call Detective Chan," Glenn shoots back. It is *his* booking sheet.

"Call whomever you like," the judge replies bluntly.

Glenn's face reddens. "I don't understand why I have to be given a difficult time on this. He is part of this investigation."

Judge Fried tells him that he is not trying to give the defense lawyer a hard time. He is trying to follow the law. A witness can only testify to facts based on his own knowledge. Otherwise it is hearsay.

Back before the jury, Glenn pulls himself together and pointedly says to the detective, "Now, I was about to show you an online booking sheet."

Judge Fried quickly jumps in: "Do you have personal knowledge of how old the defendant is?"

"No, sir."

"Next question."

Glenn is determined. The tension in the room is as thick as smoke. Glenn hunts for the proper wording that will put this issue in evidence. Fourth attempt: "Did you ever become *aware* of his age?"

The detective leans forward, smiling. Judge Fried abruptly rephrases. "Do you have *personal knowledge* of how old Johnny Ding is?"

"Not at this time, sir." The detective leans back in his chair.

"Next question," says the judge.

Fifth attempt: "Is there anything that would *refresh your memory* as to what you knew about Johnny Ding's age when he was arrested?" Sighs from the jurors.

Leemie objects, but the judge allows this question. "Back to the online booking sheet, sir," Hayman replies, trying to hold back laughter.

The judge has heard enough. "I am only going to permit the witness to testify to his own personal knowledge. Let's go on, please." By now

> **HEARSAY:**
> The witness cannot repeat conversations that he or she heard about from a third party, with certain exceptions.

Detectives Hayman Goon and David Chan.

Glenn has gone as far as he can with this witness and the jury is restless. "No further questions."

After the trial Detective Goon says, "I tried to be one step ahead of him. Once I knew what he was after, I was more at ease because I didn't think he could hurt our case." His partner, Dave, adds, "Defense attorneys got their jobs to do. They try to trip us up on any inconsistencies. We really have to think about what he's trying to get out of us. We realize that they are not malicious—unless they outright accuse us of some kind of corruption or something like that. We know what the D.A. is going to come at us with—basically it's everything we investigated. District attorneys and the detectives work together, like the TV show *Law and Order*."

In spite of the objections and interruptions, Glenn is happy with this witness. He says, "When Leemie put on her presentation, this material was all absent. She used cops who had limited involvement in the investigation of the case as a way to prevent me from developing inconsistencies. This is good strategy on her part. But still, I managed to get the inconsistencies on the record. From my vantage point, Goon was powerful."

CROSS-EXAMINATION

Walking toward the witness, Leemie says, "Good afternoon, Detective Goon." She is warm and friendly. "We've actually worked together on this case. Is that correct?"

"Yes," he says. His voice is softer now. Through Leemie's questions, Detective Goon tells the court that he spoke to Mr. Wang the day after he was released. He was upset, emotional, afraid, babbling.

"You never asked detailed questions?" Leemie asks him.

"I tried," he tells her, leaning forward again, implying his lack of success in getting details.

Leemie develops the theory that as the case progressed, the facts emerging took many twists and turns. Indeed, it was only recently that law enforcement learned the identities of all the perpetrators.

REDIRECT

"This case took a lot of twists and turns," Glenn says, picking up Leemie's phrase. Pointedly he adds, "The biggest twist and turn was Johnny Ding's cooperation."

"I don't know," the detective replies. That's all Glenn needed the jury to hear.

Once the detective is excused from the witness stand, the jurors are dismissed. Glenn says, "Goon answered everything I wanted him to answer." Glenn looks at his client, surrounded by armed officers, and repeats, "Goon was great for me."

TIME: SIX DAYS EARLIER. LATE AT NIGHT
PLACE: GLENN GARBER'S OFFICE

It was another all-nighter. This time Glenn had a meeting with Suzy Ling, Joe Chen's estranged girlfriend. She told Glenn that she did not want to testify. "It's over between him and me. I don't want to do this."

But Glenn is convinced that Suzy will be another powerful witness, especially because she is estranged from Joe Chen. "If I can show that they are no longer a couple," he explains later, "the jury will not think that she is lying to save him." Leemie will cross-examine Suzy using the same themes Glenn used when he cross-examined Echo, Johnny Ding's girlfriend: stand by your man. Glenn cannot let this happen.

Like Echo, Suzy Ling is an illegal alien. If she comes forward and testifies against the government's interests, she's afraid they could take revenge by deporting her.

Nevertheless, Glenn somehow managed to convince her to testify for Joe Chen.

Glenn and Suzy Ling worked late into the night, reviewing every possible question Leemie might throw at her during the cross-examination. By the end of their session, Glenn was certain that Suzy was ready. She will be a great witness for the defense of Joe Chen.

WITNESS FOR THE DEFENSE

- GLENN REVEALS THE NAME OF HIS MYSTERY WITNESS.
- JOE CHEN'S GIRLFRIEND IS THE STAR WITNESS FOR THE DEFENSE.
- LEEMIE CROSS-EXAMINES THE WITNESS.

DATE: TUESDAY, APRIL 28, 1998; 3:00 P.M.
PLACE: JUDGE FRIED'S COURTROOM

The time has finally come for Glenn to reveal the name of his mystery witness. Without the jury present, Glenn announces formally, "Your Honor, the witness that I intended to call goes by the name Stick. This is an individual whose name has come up throughout the trial. He was smuggled to the States along with the two confessed kidnappers, Sonny Chen and Jane Ding, as well as their victim, Mr. Wang." (Remember, Mr. Wang testified that while he was held captive he thought that he recognized Stick's voice.)

Glenn wants Stick as a witness because he was present during part of the kidnapping and could shed light on some of the facts.

Glenn says, "Stick was supposed to be in my office at one o'clock. He did not show up." Glenn says that Stick is nervous because he is subject to arrest for his involvement in this kidnapping. To protect his rights, Glenn asks that a court-appointed lawyer be assigned to him. Because Glenn is Joe Chen's lawyer, it would be a conflict of interest to represent Stick as well. Furthermore, Glenn, who is always suspicious about the state's actions, wants this court-appointed lawyer to meet Stick in a secret place—a place unknown to law enforcement.

Judge Fried asks Leemie if this witness is subject to arrest.

"Yes, judge," she replies. Law enforcement would love to get Stick.

Judge Fried signs a subpoena forcing Stick to appear. Then he arranges for a translator and a lawyer to represent this witness. He gives Glenn till the next morning to see if Stick will show up. In the meantime, the judge wants Glenn to continue with his other witnesses.

None of these precautions matter, because Stick has disappeared.

Next.

Glenn wants an additional witness, Detective Dave Chan. Leemie is against it. She says that Glenn is re-calling the detective, her witness, only to talk about the participants' ages again—and that's not relevant. Leemie later explains, "When a direct examination goes smoothly, you don't want anything to disturb it. Things could come up that, even though they are not particularly relevant, the defense might try to make into a big deal. It's not as if Dave will come on the stand and say, 'Oh, yeah, I remember now, Joe Chen didn't do it.' It's not going to be anything catastrophic, but still, a person's recollection can change slightly. Those little changes can chip away at the case. Dave's testimony went smoothly and I did not want to disturb it."

Glenn says that the participants' ages are indeed relevant. Johnny Ding is older than Joe Chen. According to Leemie's earlier reasoning, the dailo is always the oldest. That means that Johnny Ding is the leader of the kidnappers.

"You did raise the cultural relationships," the judge reminds Leemie.

"Only among relatives does age count," replies Leemie. "Johnny Ding is not related to Joe Chen."

The judge leans back in his seat, taking a moment to ponder the arguments. "Speculation," he says, agreeing with Leemie.

Glenn's face reddens. He shifts his weight from side to side. "There's a double standard here," he complains. "As I see it, the exact same point that she utilized, I can't."

Leemie claims that there is a difference between family hierarchy and gang hierarchy. If Glenn argues that they are equal, Leemie wants an opportunity to bring on an expert witness to prove him wrong.

"Does the State have an expert witness about Asian gangs?" the judge asks.

"Pardon me?" she says, thrown by the question. Collecting herself, she says that she could get an expert by this afternoon.

Ruling: The defense can include the ages of the kidnappers and the prosecutor can bring in her expert. Neither lawyer is happy. Are they both bluffing? Is the judge calling their bluffs? No one will say.

It's Glenn's move in this high-stakes poker game. He asks for yet another continuance because he needs time to interview his *own* expert to rebut her expert. "And since I do not have the resources that she has, I will need at least two or three days to get an adequate expert."

Judge Fried stops them both. "I'm going back! I am precluding the age. According to the testimony already developed, age is not relevant between Johnny Ding and the defendant. The point that Johnny Ding must be the leader simply because he is older than the defendant is pure speculation." Glenn is about to speak, but the judge has the final word. "I'm not going to allow any further arguments on this. I have made a ruling!" Everyone is tense. Glenn withdraws the detective's name from the witness list. Leemie marches to her seat. Joe Chen is silent. The jury enters.

"THE DEFENSE CALLS SUZY LING"

At first glance Suzy Ling is gorgeous, dressed in a long silk skirt, black sleeveless blouse, and sandals. She has high cheekbones, very long legs, and very, very long hair—hair falling well below her waist. Look again. Her eyes are deep black holes—dead eyes.

Suzy is on the stand to show that Joe Chen did not live in the apartment on Rivington Street during the time of the kidnapping. He lived with her.

Mary Cassidy administers the oath and Glenn begins his direct examination by asking questions about Suzy's life.

Suzy tells the court that she is twenty-eight years old and a high school graduate. In 1993 her family paid a snake head $30,000 to smuggle her to Los Angeles. It was there she met Joe Chen. When he moved to New York, she went with him. For a while she was a hostess in a restaurant. Then she worked at a massage parlor. "I work there now," she says dully. "I've been arrested and convicted for prostitution. When that happened, I gave the police different names."

Glenn asks the witness about her current relationship with Joe Chen. He wants the record to show that the witness and his client are no longer a couple, and therefore Suzy Ling has no reason to lie to protect him. Searching for a dramatic presentation, Glenn takes a moment to talk quietly to his client. He twirls toward the witness. "Has Joe Chen been in jail for the last ten months?" Up until this time everyone has been careful not to let the jury know that the defendant has been imprisoned. The knowledge of the incarceration might have a psychological effect on the jury that could be prejudicial.

"Yes," she replies simply. The jurors do not seem surprised.

Later Glenn explains why he asked this question. "I figured it didn't matter at this point. There was enough bad stuff coming out against him. And I may create some sympathy for him."

Suzy tells the court that when Joe Chen was arrested, she visited him one or two times a week. She spoke to him on the telephone until three months ago, when she decided to end the relationship. He still calls her, but sometimes she doesn't answer the phone.

"Do you feel uncomfortable being involved with this?"

"Objection!" shouts the prosecutor. Leemie anticipates that Glenn's line of questioning implies that Suzy Ling's "discomfort" is in seeing the prosecutor, Leemie, watching her every move. His next question will suggest that the prosecutor interrogated Suzy Ling while Glenn was waiting to interview her. Leemie insists that that is not true.

The judge allows Glenn's question and Suzy answers no, she is not uncomfortable.

Since the night Suzy was with the prosecutor when she was supposed to go over the defense, Glenn has been resentful. He won't let the issue drop.

"Did you see *this woman* there when you went to the D.A.'s office?" he says loudly, thrusting his arm toward the prosecutor. Leemie sits quietly at the table, listening to the testimony.

Suzy tells the court that she was in the assistant district attorney's office from noon to eight P.M. and that she was questioned about the kidnapping. Glenn glares at Leemie. Then, with a nod to the jurors, he moves on to a new line of questioning.

Earlier Glenn carefully prepped Suzy to speak truthfully, but say very limited things about the apartment where the kidnappers were held. For instance, she told Glenn that she never saw Joe Chen at the apartment—he wasn't living there. At first her testimony is exactly as Glenn expected. She says that in the early part of 1995 she lived with Joe Chen at the Rivington Street apartment. In June they moved out. They returned to pick up some of her belongings that were left behind in the back bedroom. She was in the apartment for about ten minutes.

"Was the front bedroom door open or closed?" Glenn asks.

"Open," she says. That means she had to have seen the victims who were chained to the window grate in the front bedroom. Then, in front of the judge, the jury, the prosecutor, and her ex-boyfriend, Suzy Ling changes her testimony from what she had told Glenn. "After I left, Joe Chen stayed. A few of them were talking."

Leemie sits up.

Glenn's mouth drops. "Oh, no!" he says to himself, afraid that his entire case is about to unravel. This presumably innocent remark puts the defendant smack dab in the middle of the crime. Why would Joe stay? What was he doing there?

He tries to pull her back to the areas they discussed last night. Glenn doesn't even have to look over at the prosecutor's desk; he knows that Leemie is busy writing notes.

"Did you go back there?" he asks her, trying to get her back on track.

"Two days later, to get more things."

"Who was there?" Suzy says that she only saw Johnny Ding and his girlfriend at the apartment.

"See him making telephone calls?"

"No."

"Did you see the victims of the kidnapping in handcuffs or—"

"No, I did not. I did not!" But the victims said that more than once they saw a woman with very long hair. "Move on! Move on!" A voice howls in Glenn's head. He must get her off the stand. "I have no further questions."

. . .

Before Leemie's cross-examination, Judge Fried calls the lawyers to the side. He checks that Glenn still wants him to instruct the jury after Leemie's cross concerning the time Joe Chen beat his girlfriend. Glenn prefers to make the decision after the cross.

"Judge, let me ask a couple more questions," Glenn adds.

"Sure."

He returns to Suzy. "You have come to my office only to talk about your testimony?"

"Yes."

"Did I ever tell you to lie?" Lawyers often ask this question so that the jury hears that they would never ask witnesses to lie.

"No."

"I have no further questions."

CROSS-EXAMINATION

First Leemie wants to clear up the reason a police officer brought Suzy Ling to her office. Second she wants to prove that Suzy is not afraid to testify in front of the prosecutor.

Leemie approaches the witness with the following questions that call for yes or no answers. "You remember who I am. Right?" she asks sweetly. "In fact we met face-to-face last Monday. Right? . . . The person who asked you to come here is Police Officer Tsoi? . . . He was the police officer who arrested certain individuals for a robbery at your massage parlor. . . . On that robbery case you met with another assistant district attorney who was a man. Right? . . . You testified at the grand jury on that?"

"Yes. Yes. Yes. Yes. Yes. Yes."

"Officer Tsoi asked you to come down to the district attorney's office last Monday?"

"Uh-huh."

"Just for the record, if you could say 'yes' or 'no,' because the stenographer can't really write down what 'uh-huh' is."

"Okay. I won't 'uh-huh' anymore." Three jurors giggle.

All along Leemie has insisted that she spoke with Suzy in her office for a very short time and then went off to court. Afterward, Leemie explains why it was a short time: "During the time that Suzy Ling was in my office, she adamantly denied that she was even in the kidnappers' apartment. Mostly, I think, she was afraid of being implicated in this crime. For her to say, 'Yes, he was there at certain times,' or 'Yes, I was there and saw such-and-such,' might be seen as an admission of guilt. She was not going to do that, no matter what."

After Suzy says that she waited at length for the prosecutor to return from court, Leemie moves on to the relationship between the witness and the defendant. Leemie explains afterward, "Once I realized I wasn't going to get anything more about the kidnappings from her, I tried to get information about her relationship with Joe Chen. I was looking for any motive she might have for protecting him. I asked about other bad acts that she might have committed for him because I wanted to show that she would do anything to help her boyfriend, including lie on the witness stand."

Always meticulous about laying the foundation for her future questions, Leemie first asks Suzy to point out Joe Chen by identifying an article of clothing that he is wearing.

"He's wearing a black-colored suit."

The judge looks up. "What color suit?"

"Black."

Judge Fried asks her to describe another article of clothing.

"He's wearing a white color shirt and a flowery tie."

Leemie is trying hard not to laugh. "Well, judge, that is actually Mr. Garber." Everyone is laughing, even Glenn. Not quite everyone—Joe Chen does not laugh.

Judge Fried suggests that the witness turn around and face the table. "Do you see him at that table?" Suzy describes her ex-boyfriend as the one with glasses. Leemie moves on.

During the summer of 1995, Suzy Ling worked at a massage parlor from noon to midnight. Sometimes, though, when business was slow, she went home early. At that time Joe Chen was not working. Suzy testifies that when Mr. Wang and Mr. Li were first kidnapped, Joe Chen was not in her apartment when she returned home, even though he did not have a day job. She readily tells the court, "Oh, at night he always returned."

"Stop! Stop! Stop!" thinks Glenn, looking straight ahead.

But Leemie does not stop. "Is Joe Chen the only person you know in America?"

"Who did I say that to?" Suzy didn't practice this question.

"Okay. I will make it clear. You have no other relatives other than your boyfriend?"

"That's right. Yes."

"Didn't you come to his earlier court appearance?" [This refers to the pretrial hearing to suppress Joe Chen's two statements.]

"Oh, no," Glenn thinks, "she is building the relationship I so carefully tore apart."

"Yes, that's right," Suzy answers.

Leemie digs deeper, soliciting the very information she was prepared to obtain from Joe Chen if he chose to testify. "In November of 1995, the defendant hit you at your apartment."

"Right."

"You pressed charges with the police on November 20, 1995?"

"I don't remember the date."

"But after that you never came to court?"

"I didn't went to court." Instead, Suzy protected her boyfriend.

By the end of the day's testimony, Leemie manages to get into evidence a prior bad act committed by Joe Chen (hitting his girlfriend) that suggests he is a violent person. She manages to get into evidence the fact that Joe was not working and was not always home with his girlfriend. What was Joe doing all day? Was he with the kidnappers? The answers to Leemie's questions, coupled with the perfect statement *"After I left, Joe Chen stayed,"* are all the prosecutor needs. No further questions.

The best thing Glenn can do for his client is get Suzy Ling off the stand. "I have no questions," he tells the court.

Suzy is dismissed with a "Thank you" from the judge. She appears to have no idea of the debacle that just took place. But then, maybe she planned it.

.   .   .

The trial is moving faster than Judge Fried anticipated. "I think there's an 80 percent possibility that this case is going to be completely finished by tomorrow," he tells the jury. "If I'm correct, I will then charge you after lunch. I am hoping you can begin your deliberations right then."

A hand goes up in the jury box. "Does that mean that we are going to be sequestered if—"

"If you deliberate tomorrow, and you are unable to reach a verdict, there's a possibility you may be sequestered," the judge says.

"See you tomorrow at ten o'clock. Please be here promptly so we can begin promptly. Have a pleasant evening. Do not discuss the case."

CHARGING THE JURY:
The judge instructs the jury on the rules of law that apply to the case they are about to deliberate.

Judge Fried gives both lawyers a draft of his charge to the jury, and they plan to meet the following morning, after Glenn has a chance to look over the material.

Glenn talks briefly with his client before he is taken back to his cell. He packs his notes into his well-worn briefcase. "I want to go home, see my family, and work on my summation. I am working on three hours' sleep. I can't function anymore." He shakes his head and sighs. "She was terrible up there. I can't believe I put her on the stand."

Leemie leans across the aisle. "At least you didn't redirect." Glenn shakes his head and walks out of the courtroom.

> **JUDGE FRIED SAYS:**
> Both lawyers are entitled to review and discuss the judge's charge to the jury before they give their summations.

RING OF TRUTH

- THE DEFENSE RESTS.
- GLENN AND LEEMIE DELIVER THEIR CLOSING ARGUMENTS.

TIME: WEDNESDAY, APRIL 29, 1998; 9:15 A.M.
PLACE: JUDGE FRIED'S COURTROOM

Closing statements—the summation—the last chance, the ninth inning, the final round. Glenn is working on two hours' sleep; Leemie was up all night.

Leemie says that she couldn't sleep because her mind was racing: "What am I missing?...What should I say differently?" Before the jury enters the courtroom, she rereads her notes, even though she largely memorized her summation days ago.

"I write out my summation and then outline what points I want to hit. After that I make a chart: on one side I write every argument that Glenn

> **CLOSING STATEMENTS (SUMMATION):**
> A summation consists of the lawyer's interpretation of the evidence presented throughout the trial. This is the last time the lawyers argue their views before the jury.

might make, on the other side I try to rebut those arguments. It's a lot of writing."

Glenn says that he first writes a free-flowing speech, then he edits it, highlighting the areas that he thinks important. "Afterward, I memorize it so that I will be able to look directly at the jury while I'm speaking. I plan my facial gestures and inflections, a lower voice to describe complicated issues, and a higher one to point out inconsistencies. I practice my speech in front of my wife. She coaches me."

The case is about to resume. Two guards escort Joe Chen to the defense table. He smiles sheepishly and mouths "Good morning."

Since Stick has disappeared, Glenn has no other witnesses. Once again he asks for a continuance so that he can search for Stick. But Judge Fried will not adjourn the trial at this late date. Besides, it is unlikely that he will find Stick.

Glenn later says that he asked for a continuance to get it on the record. If Joe is found guilty, this could be another issue for his appeal.

. . .

At ten o'clock the jurors enter the courtroom carrying suitcases and knapsacks. If they cannot reach a verdict today, they will be sequestered.

The jury is no longer a shy, passive group of strangers. They seem jumpy, like athletes warming up before a game.

"We're ready to continue," the judge tells them.

"I think I'm going to throw up," Leemie whispers.

Leemie and Glenn go through the formality of resting their cases. "The defense rests." Glenn's voice is strong. "The People rest," Leemie says softly.

> **JUDGE FRIED SAYS:**
> In New York State the defendant has the right to a sequestered jury. Isolating the jury in this manner prevents jury tampering.

Summations are given in the reverse order of opening statements. That means Glenn goes first.

"One word of caution," the judge advises the jury. "What is said in a closing statement is not evidence. Evidence comes from the mouths of the witnesses, the stipulations, and the documents. With that introduction, Mr. Garber, you may proceed."

. . .

Glenn presumes that he has lost the support of the jury. "They were frustrated by the difficulties during my questioning." This is his chance to win them back. Glenn places his notes on a wooden lectern in front of the jury. "Good morning, ladies and gentlemen," he says, smiling.

"Good morning." They smile back.

At first Glenn is hesitant; his voice wavers. But as he proceeds, he becomes steadier. "I have an opportunity to tell you what I believe the evidence shows in this case," he says. "The critical point was the claim by Johnny and Jane Ding that Joe Chen is the leader of the kidnappings. From that foundation, Assistant Kahng built her case. I submit to you that this foundation is unreliable."

Item by item, Glenn takes the jury through the evidence: the time of the arrests, the mistaken identifications, the government's agreements with the cooperating witnesses, and the ulterior motives behind the testimonies—all the inconsistencies that he tried to bring out during his cross-examinations. He focuses on a few jurors whom he thinks have been sympathetic. "There is no real indication that there is a dailo out there, with a cellular phone, with a girlfriend with long hair," he says, waving his fingers in the air.

One by one he challenges the motives and the sincerity of Leemie's witnesses. First, the detectives of the Major Case Squad. Glenn reports that during an interrogation, the detectives told Joe Chen that the confessed kidnappers had already implicated him in the crime. "They wanted to see how he was going to respond to that. It's a very effective interrogation tool. They also used it on Johnny Ding.

"Is it a coincidence," he asks, moving onto the cooperating witnesses, "that Jane Ding just *happens* to come clean and implicate Joe Chen ten days after Johnny Ding makes a better deal with the government?" He tilts his head. "It doesn't make sense that she just happened to come clean. She wanted a better deal."

Glenn reminds the jury of Jane's behavior during his cross-examination. "She claimed not to understand much. She's not as innocent and pure as she appears to be. She finagled the deal of the century when she implicated Joe Chen." He moves away from the lectern, his hand caressing his heart like a crooner singing to his sweetheart. "In addition to saying, 'Oh, my heart is heavy,' and all that crap, she said the reason why she didn't initially implicate Joe Chen was because she loves his brother."

Leemie perks up, surprised that Glenn would use the word "crap" when addressing the jury. By now Glenn has made eye contact with all the jurors. "But during an initial interview with the police, she had no problem telling them that Joe Chen was involved in other criminal activity."

As far as the defense is concerned, the only truthful testimonies are those of the two victims, Mr. Wang and Mr. Li. But they, too, are somewhat suspect. They only mentioned the incidents that helped the prosecutor's case. "These victims were blindfolded and couldn't see the leader, but they claimed that they were able to see the hair and legs of the dailo's girlfriend. Why couldn't they see the legs of the dailo? Joe Chen walks with a limp, but they don't say that."

Glenn admits that Joe Chen's girlfriend, Suzy Ling, was not a good witness for the defense. But the reason she wasn't good was that she turned on Joe and decided to cooperate with the D.A.'s office. "After all, she spoke with *them* in the middle of the trial," he says, looking over at Leemie, who is editing her notes. "She has a better rapport with Leemie Kahng than she does with me."

On to Echo, Johnny Ding's girlfriend. He wants to defuse Echo's testimony before Leemie has the chance to build it up. "She says she lived with him [Johnny Ding] for over four years, and yet she doesn't know anything about his criminal activities. That's a bit odd. This guy is a one-man crime wave. He is extorting people. He's beating people. He is doing all sorts of terrible things. It just doesn't make sense. Either she's afraid of him, or she's trying to help him." He pauses. "Maybe she's afraid of the government, because she's an illegal alien."

Joe Chen's statement when interrogated is Leemie's most powerful evidence. Glenn must turn it to his client's advantage. He stresses the fact that Joe Chen consistently denied his participation in this crime. "He pleaded with the D.A. and the detectives when they were interrogating him. *'Please believe me, I was just there. I did not participate in this case.'* There is no evidence of high-enough quality to counter this statement.

"The bottom line is: The case is founded on the word of Jane Ding and Johnny Ding—the bad dude—and you cannot rely on them when you make a decision of this importance."

Glenn has been talking for forty-five minutes. As he nears the end of his summation, he takes a deep breath and looks at every juror. "This is one of the most important decisions you're ever going to make about another individual. I submit to you, ladies and gentlemen, that the foundation given you by the prosecution is just not enough. They have not proven their case beyond a reasonable doubt. I ask you to acquit Joe Chen. Thank you."

Glenn Garber returns to the defense table, unbuttons his jacket, and puts his arm around Chen.

· · ·

"The exact same instructions that I gave you with regard to Mr. Garber's summation apply to Ms. Kahng," Judge Fried announces. "You may proceed."

Leemie sets up a stand with the evidence photographs of the kidnapper's apartment and the chart with Chinese names and nicknames, visual reminders of the crime.

Earlier, during the trial, when Glenn was cross-examining Jane Ding, he made a comment about truth: "*I am not asking about the truth at this time.*" Straightaway, Leemie knew that she would include that line in her summation. Now, she opens with it.

"During the height of the cross-examination of Jane Ding, Mr. Garber yelled out, 'I am not asking about the truth at this time.' Do you recall that?"

Glenn curses Leemie under his breath.

"Now, I think he tried to clarify it a little bit later," Leemie qualifies the comment. "Maybe he misspoke—perhaps it was a slip—a Freudian slip—but it was very telling, because he knows what the truth is." (Glenn's fist clenches. "She's trying to use me, get into my head, announcing that I think my client is guilty.") "Maybe he doesn't want to hear that his defendant, Joe Chen, is the dailo, the mastermind of this kidnapping, the man with the cell phone. That's the truth."

Leemie pauses to thank the jury for their patience and for being so attentive. Then she says, "I'd like to do a little building with you. I'd like to build blocks of a pyramid, a pyramid of truth, which will prove the defendant's guilt beyond a reasonable doubt."

For the next two hours Leemie takes the jury through the trial. She's nervous. She falls back into her opening argument, uttering the mantra

You will hear... before every sentence. "You will hear that soon after the victim was blindfolded and beaten, he was forced to make phone calls to his family in China.... You will hear evidence that this defendant was the person with the cell phone."

The judge gently reminds her that this is closing argument, not the opening. Leemie blushes, apologizes, and continues her speech.

"Although Mr. Garber kept saying that the foundation of the People's case rests on informants and accomplices, that, in fact, is not true."

Leemie's first building block is the two victims' testimonies. A kidnapping occurred, there's no doubt about that. Her second block is—as Glenn expected—Joe Chen's interrogation statement. "Mr. Garber said that the evidence shows Jane Ding as the key player in the kidnappings. But the defendant said, '*Jane Ding was told to bring the man back to the apartment.*' That directly contradicts Mr. Garber's argument that she somehow orchestrated the kidnappings."

Leemie pauses to look at the jurors. "Now, isn't it funny how the defendant knows that?" Another pause. "He remembers incredible details of what happened, including the planning."

Line by line she picks apart Joe Chen's statement. " '*I saw Johnny Ding bring another man out of the rest room. It was not the same man from four days ago.*' Earlier, he said that he only saw the back of Mr. Wang. How does he know that this other man is a different one when he only saw a back?

" '*I did not know what they were doing at the time. My concern was the apartment.*' This guy goes to his apartment. His brother, his cousin, and Johnny Ding have men bound and blindfolded. Yet he is not concerned? Does that ring of truth?"

Leemie mentions the dailo. "Objection," Glenn says, revisiting the fight about the dailo's obligation to take care of family members. Although objections during opening and closing arguments are, out of professional courtesy, rarely used, they are not forbidden.

Judge Fried rules that Leemie can make the argument that the elder person is supposed to care for his younger brother. Though irked by the loss of momentum, Leemie calmly moves on to the second victim's $8,000 ransom. "How would the defendant remember $8,000? He sees all these things, and he hears all these things, because he took part in them."

Leemie raises her next building block, the corroborating evidence: Joe Chen's telephone records.

"If you don't think that this is enough, if you don't think that the defendant's virtual admission is enough, and that the phone records are enough, there is another block—the testimony of Johnny Ding's girlfriend, Miss Echo. Her testimony is crucial. She said that she saw the defendant order his younger brother to beat one of the victims.

"I can't really say anything about her relationship with Johnny Ding. Johnny Ding is a bad guy." She looks at the defense attorney. "Mr. Garber, and Johnny Ding himself, made that clear. But he sheltered his girlfriend from all these activities. And he got so angry when he found out that—"

"Objection," shouts Glenn. Leemie can't vouch for a witness's credibility. Leemie's statement implies that she believes Johnny Ding was indeed angered by this.

"Overruled." Judge Fried gives the lawyers a great deal of leeway in drawing reasonable inferences from the evidence during closing arguments.

"Mr. Li told his girlfriend that Johnny Ding tricked him into the apartment. He actually beat Mr. Li because he didn't want his girlfriend to know.

"I don't think it's incredible that she didn't know about all his activities," Leemie says in rebuttal of Glenn's earlier statement. "She worked until nighttime. And who can really say about love? Who can judge love?

"Mr. Garber asks you to speculate. 'Maybe this happened—maybe that happened.' He is kicking sand around this pyramid of truth, trying to distract you from what the truth is. Remember, he is not asking about the truth at this time." You can almost see steam rising from Glenn's head, he's so angry. Leemie will not back down.

"Block after block after block. Big blocks of evidence that include the victims' testimony, the defendant's admission, the phone records, and Miss Echo's testimony."

Pacing back and forth in front of the jurors, she repeats, "Mr. Garber said that the foundation of the People's case rests on the accomplices. This is untrue. What the accomplices do is fill in evidence, they make things clearer, they make things fit. Unfortunately, the People can't pick nuns and priests as our witnesses." She crosses her arms around her waist. "Wouldn't we all love that?" she asks casually. "Jane Ding is not a nun, and Johnny Ding is far from a priest."

Leemie says that the standard for the support needed for an accomplice's testimony is low. "All you have to do is be satisfied that the other evidence *tends to connect* the defendant with the commission of the crime. 'Tends to connect'—that's very important."

Meanwhile, Glenn, fuming from Leemie's "kicking sand" comment, objects once again. He asks to approach the bench. The judge sends the jury out for a well-needed break while he listens to Glenn's objection.

"I didn't want to do this in front of the jury out of respect for her," Glenn nods toward Leemie, "but I move for a mistrial, based on the personal characterizations that she has made throughout the closing arguments.

"She keeps referring to my comment about not asking about the truth. She is twisting what happened, implying I tried to lead the witness into a lie. *The truth! The truth! The truth!* I was not trying to hide the truth in any way, I was trying to direct the witness by my questions. That was the intent of my statement. In essence, she is saying that I have no integrity. I'm a liar. Therefore, the jury should disbelieve what I am saying."

Leemie reminds His Honor that after she mentioned the "truth" statement, she conceded that he "clarified it."

"That's correct, you did," says Judge Fried.

Glenn whirls at her, "You said, 'He tried to distance himself from it.'" Then he calms down and looks at the judge, palms raised. "That was basically what she said."

But the judge denies a mistrial, the jurors return, and Leemie continues. "I'll try not to be too much longer," she tells the curious jurors, who by now have a pretty good idea that the lawyers are again at each other. "If you will just bear with me, I want to make sure there was nothing left out. Thank you very much again."

Leemie will not let Glenn's objections intimidate her. On the contrary, they make her bolder, a lioness protecting her cub-victims. "Mr. Garber started out by saying the accomplices are not credible. Then he says that the detectives of the *elite* Major Case Squad—who have no motive to lie against this defendant—all of a sudden, in Mr. Garber's eyes, are suspect. And then, you know what? The victims *themselves* are suspect. Everybody lied. This is some grand conspiracy against the defendant." She's shaking her hand toward Joe Chen.

"I submit to you, it defies logic. It makes no sense whatsoever. And this conspiracy theory is not as accurate as the evidence that was presented to you."

Glenn objects a fourth time, the judge overrules him, and Leemie shifts to Johnny Ding's and Jane Ding's motives for telling the truth, namely, that if they are caught lying, they will lose their government agreements and end up with more time in prison. Leemie stares, defiantly, at the defense attorney. "And as Mr. Garber pointed out, Mr. Johnny Ding is a very self-interested person.

"Which brings me to Suzy Ling." Leemie saves Joe Chen's girl-friend's damaging statements for last, reminding the jury of their violent relationship and of her statement about leaving Joe behind when they visited the kidnapping apartment.

Leemie's "pyramid of truth" is complete. "I ask that you deliberate conscientiously and come back with a verdict of guilty on all of the charges and all the counts against *that* defendant, Joe Chen. Thank you."

.   .   .

As soon as Leemie sits down, she begins to second-guess herself. *I should have said this. I should have said that.* "It's now in the jury's hands. There is nothing more I can bring to them. Nothing more I can do." She says that she feels powerless.

Judge Fried asks, "Anything further before we recess? Mr. Garber?"

Glenn has plenty to say. Again, he moves for a mistrial, declaring, "She shifted the burden." Remember, the burden of proving a case beyond a reasonable doubt rests solely on the prosecutor. The defense does not have to come forward with evidence. "At one point in Leemie's summation, she told the jury that there was no evidence of an argument between Joe Chen and Johnny Ding. But there *was* evidence. Johnny Ding said that they had a fight in a restaurant. So not only is it a mischaracterization, but it also improperly shifts the burden to me when it legally remains on her. She created a scenario in which she said something happened that would require an explanation from me."

"The application for a mistrial is denied. We will resume at precisely two-fifteen. Have a pleasant lunch, counselors."

WE SIT TOGETHER AS JUDGES

- JUDGE FRIED INSTRUCTS THE JURY.
- THE JURY DELIBERATES THE FATE OF JOE CHEN.

TIME: WEDNESDAY, APRIL 29, 1998; 1:30 P.M.
PLACE: A RESTAURANT IN CHINATOWN

"I think juries are terrific," Judge Fried says during the lunch break. "They have a collective intelligence that is better than any of us who try cases. They give up their own time to perform a very important civic duty. It's right up there with voting and serving in the military."

Judge Fried likens a trial to baking a cake. "You need all the ingredients to bake a cake. If you leave one out, no cake. This is true of a criminal trial as well. Sometimes a crime has two ingredients; other times, more. For example, a murder has two ingredients. Ingredient one, the person intended to cause the death of another human being. Ingredient two, the person did indeed cause the death. In American law you have to prove both ingredients beyond a reasonable doubt to get a guilty verdict. If you can't, the defendant is found not guilty."

JURY CHARGE

Back in court, Judge Fried describes the general principles of all criminal cases to the jury. The jurors listen carefully as the judge, standing by his raised desk (the bench), begins his instruction.

> *You have agreed, under oath, to accept without hesitation, and without reservation, the principles that I am about to state. I expect you will adhere to the oath that you have taken, or else there will not be a fair trial.*

Three jurors nod their heads in agreement. The judge pauses to gaze at his jury, his admirable jury, who have listened so patiently, so carefully, for three long weeks.

> *We sit together as judges. You are the sole and exclusive judge of the facts. You should decide this case coolly, calmly, deliberately, without fear, without favor, without sympathy. It is your sworn duty to decide the guilt or nonguilt of this defendant, based on the evidence—and solely on the evidence—that you heard and saw during the course of this trial, and for no other reason.*

Leemie and Glenn do not interrupt the judge's talk. That would be considered much too discourteous. Besides, they've already reviewed, edited, and approved these instructions.

Judge Fried explains that the jurors may not engage in guesswork or speculation. They may not consider anything outside of the evidence. They may not play detective. All the testimony struck from the record must be "totally, completely, and wholly disregarded."

The jurors must decide for themselves just how believable each witness is. The judge suggests a number of commonsense guidelines: the witness's knowledge of the facts, their motive for testifying, their intelligence, their education. "Ask yourself a series of questions: Did the witness appear to be neutral and trustworthy, friendly, frank, and reliable? Did the witness appear to be hostile, prejudiced, or reveal a reason not to tell the truth?"

THE PRESUMPTION OF INNOCENCE

The judge says that the presumption of innocence applies to every single criminal case tried in this country. "You must keep it in mind throughout your deliberations. The presumption of innocence exists in this room at this very moment, and it will accompany you into the jury room. The only way it can be destroyed is by *all* of you agreeing, based on the evidence, and for no other reason, that the defendant is guilty, and that he has been proven guilty beyond a reasonable doubt."

He also reminds the jury that they "may not draw any unfavorable conclusions from the fact that the defendant did not testify." They must disregard this fact entirely.

.   .   .

Pausing to sip water, the judge invites the jury to stand and stretch before he moves into the actual charges against Joe Chen.

Once the jurors are settled back in their seats, the judge reviews the particular charges against the defendant. Legal definitions come into play: "abduct," "physical injury," "serious physical injury," "ransom."

The only voice is that of the judge. Everyone else is silent, attentive to his every word. The awesome power of the law, the awesome power of twelve citizens deciding the fate of another human being, penetrates the room. You can feel it, taste it.

An hour goes by. The judge gives more definitions: "extortion," "larceny," "grand larceny." It's a lot to remember.

> **THE CHARGES:**
> 1. Kidnapping:
>   a. Joe Chen abducted the two victims with the intent to compel a third person to pay ransom.
>   b. Joe Chen held them for more than twelve hours with the intent to inflict physical injury on them.
> 2. Grand larceny in the second degree: Joe Chen stole their property by extortion.

Finally Judge Fried describes how to deliberate the case. Although there are no hard-and-fast rules, common sense should prevail. Jurors should give their opinion, but listen to the others as well. Since they have not been permitted to take notes, testimony must be read back to them. The forewoman will send the judge a note (there is a buzzer in the room) listing what they want to hear. Then Leemie and Glenn will go through the trial's transcript and mark pages and lines for the court stenographer to read. The jury cannot read the transcripts themselves because then they would see all the sidebar discussions that are either not relevant or could prejudice their deliberations.

"When you have a verdict, send me a note," the judge tells them. "Don't tell me what the verdict is. We'll bring you into the courtroom."

When the jurors are escorted into the jury room to begin their deliberation, Leemie sighs, "That's it. It's truly in their hands."

The wait begins. Glenn paces up and down the center aisle, constantly checking his beeper. Leemie does not move at all. Some of her colleagues drop by, squeeze her hand, and offer an empathetic smile. She says that she feels numb. Everyone waits. Everyone wonders: What is happening inside the jury room?

INSIDE THE JURY ROOM

The jury room is a small, windowless space that looks like a conference room in a slightly seedy office. The jurors sit around a large, battered conference table. The forewoman begins by asking for initial reactions. Everyone is hesitant; no one wants to talk first.

"As far as I'm concerned, Joe Chen is guilty on all counts," an elderly woman says, opening the discussion. "I feel bad for his parents." Four others raise their hands, agreeing.

Another woman, a great-grandmother, insists that he is innocent. A thirty-something, soft-spoken bearded man, who walks with a cane because of a ski accident, agrees with the great-grandmother. Not guilty. The prosecutor has not proven Joe Chen's guilt beyond a reasonable doubt.

The forewoman thinks that Joe Chen was *probably* involved in the crime, but there isn't enough evidence to find him guilty.

Five say guilty; four, not guilty. The rest are on the fence.

Eight P.M. No verdict. The jurors are driven to an undisclosed hotel somewhere in New York City. Four guards accompany them to insure that there is no jury tampering. Until they reach a verdict, they will live in a cocoon, as if they were the last people on Earth.

TIME: THURSDAY, APRIL 30, 1998; 9:25 A.M.
PLACE: JUDGE FRIED'S COURTROOM

The jurors send the judge a note. They want to hear Mr. Wang's testimony about what happened when he entered the apartment.

Judge Fried dons his black robe and heads to the courtroom. Joe Chen, his translator, the lawyers, the court clerk, and the guards are already in place. After the note is read into the record, the lawyers go to work, marking each page, each line, with stickums.

If the lawyers cannot agree about what can be read, Judge Fried will review the material and make the decision for them. "I should tell you," the judge warns the two lawyers, "I have a very expansive view of the readback. If the jurors want it, I tend to think they should get as much as we can give them."

Meanwhile a second note arrives, with a long list of readbacks. Mary passes out cookies to lighten the pressure—and boredom. Everyone but Leemie, who has no appetite, and Joe Chen, who has fallen asleep in his chair, nibbles as they wait.

Noon. Judge Fried suggests that they bring in the jury and read back the finished sections.

Twelve-twenty P.M. The jury enters. "I have your notes, ladies and gentlemen," says the judge cordially. "I apologize for what may seem to have taken longer than reasonable. The testimony is lengthy. We haven't done everything, but we'll give you what we have."

As the court stenographer reads aloud the transcript, two women jurors nod their heads to each other in recognition of the statements. Back to the deliberations.

The lawyers have their lunches delivered to the courtroom. Leemie doesn't touch her fruit salad. Glenn manages to get down half a meatball hero, but leaves french fries, onion rings, and a Coke.

Three-forty-five P.M. Two more notes. "We want to hear all the testimony about the dailo."

Six-twenty-three P.M. Once back in the jury room, a juror announces, "The readback about the dailo clarifies it for me. Guilty." Now there are six.

It's a juror's birthday. The forewoman sends Judge Fried a note asking to be dismissed early because they planned a birthday celebration. The judge, pleased that they are getting along well because it will help the deliberations go more smoothly, grants their request.

Another note: "Read-back testimony from both victims about the ransom money." Then another readback. And so it goes, on and on and on.

No sooner do they return to the jury room than yet another a note comes out. "Have you answered all our written requests so far?"

The judge smiles. "Suppose I just take this and write the word 'no' and send it back. Any objection to that, counselors?"

No objection.

By now the jury is focusing on Joe Chen's written statement. A juror later explains, "We were all very interested in his statement, because we never heard him speak." They go through the document sentence by sentence.

"Look it," a juror argues, "he actually says, 'I was there when the first man was brought in. . . . I was there when the second man was brought in.' What was he doing there?"

Another juror: "Now about that $8,000. How did he know that the closing amount was $8,000? When the second victim arrived, they asked for $10,000."

Yet another juror: "Echo said, 'I saw Joe Chen tell his brother to beat him up.' That makes him a participant. It's enough for me."

Eighth vote, "Guilty."

But the great-grandmother still says that Joe Chen is not guilty. No one can convince her to the contrary. Frustrated by the lack of consensus after two days, the birthday juror starts yelling. By now everyone is on edge, each is emotionally exhausted, and no verdict is in sight. The jurors adjourn for the party and another night at the motel.

TIME: FRIDAY, MAY 1, 1998; 10:30 A.M.
PLACE: JUDGE FRIED'S COURTROOM

The jury continues deliberating and the lawyers continue to mark the transcript for the readbacks. Joe Chen sits slumped in his chair.

Ten-thirty A.M. Another note. "We want to hear Johnny Ding's testimony and anything that mentions the blindfolds." They also want the definition of grand larceny in the second degree. Judge Fried brings them into the courtroom and explains grand larceny in the second degree. The jury goes back to their room. The lawyers return to marking Johnny Ding's testimony.

Within minutes another note arrives.

The jury has reached a verdict.

BEYOND REASONABLE DOUBT

TIME: FRIDAY, MAY 1, 1998; 11:31 A.M.
PLACE: JUDGE FRIED'S COURTROOM

"*Wait. Wait.* There are still more readbacks." Glenn begs the judge to ask if the jury wants to hear the remaining testimony.

"I intend to bring them in and accept their verdict."

Two guards go off to get the jury. Caroline Basile, the Asian gang coordinator for the district attorney's office, slides into the first row behind Leemie. Judge Fried's law clerk and his secretary come in, curious to hear the verdict. Four more guards enter and station themselves behind Joe Chen. The detectives pace in the hallway.

The months of investigation and legal maneuvering have come down to just a few minutes. The room is as silent as a tomb. This is it.

The jury enters. They look pale; some fight back tears. One juror later says, "It was really weird when we walked in to give the verdict. All of a sudden the police are standing there, more of them than usual. Glenn is smiling at us. The defendant is still looking straight ahead, like nothing was going on."

The courtroom feels as tight as a massive hot-air balloon. Caroline puts her hand to her chest to quiet the beating of her heart.

Judge Fried says, "I have a note, ladies and gentlemen, saying that you have reached a verdict." He asks them if they still want to hear the outstanding readbacks. They do not. "I am going to ask that Ms. Cassidy proceed."

"Will the foreperson please rise," says Mary, the court clerk, as she rises from her desk.

The foreperson stands. Her hand is shaking.

"Madame Foreperson, have you agreed upon a verdict?"

"Yes, we have."

Joe Chen stands and looks into the eyes of the jurors. His expression betrays no malice toward these twelve citizens. He is calm. Stoic. Glenn, still smiling, stands beside him.

"How say you as to the first count of the indictment charging the defendant with the crime of kidnapping in the first degree as to Mr. Wang Dong?"

Joe Chen's left pinky trembles violently on the edge of the table. *Tap-tap-tap-tap-tap.*

"The jury has found him guilty."

"How say you as to the second count of the indictment charging the defendant with the kidnapping in the first degree as to Mr. Li Jun?"

"The jury has found him guilty."

The next charge of kidnapping: "Guilty."

And the next one: "Guilty."

And the two charges of grand larceny: "Guilty" and "guilty."

The tension abates. It is as if the hot air is no more and the balloon lies crumpled on the ground.

Judge Fried asks the clerk to poll the jury. One by one the jurors state, "Yes, I find the defendant guilty." The court clerk gives the formal reply.

.   .   .

Glenn puts his arms around his client. Then they sit down. Through it all Leemie has not moved a hair. She is completely, utterly numb.

The judge thanks the jurors on behalf of himself and both lawyers for the careful attention they gave the case. "I observed the trial as you did. In my view the evidence more than amply justifies the verdict that you returned." Judge Fried deliberately chose the words "amply justifies," rather than "affirms" their finding. He later explains that it is not appropriate for a trial judge to tell a jury whether or not their verdict is correct. "Because I had already told the jury that they are the sole and exclusive judge of the facts, my agreeing with them is irrelevant. But their decision is a very serious matter, and I did not want them to leave feeling uncomfortable with their verdict."

He continues, "I understand that it was a juror's birthday yesterday. I wish you a happy birthday. Ladies and gentlemen, you are excused."

As they file out, juror number three pauses. He stares at the man he just convicted of the heinous crimes. Then he turns and leaves the courtroom for the last time.

Later the juror says, "It was so weird. We press the elevator button and go home, and he doesn't get to . . . you know . . . he doesn't even get to . . ." His voice trails off.

. . .

Soon after the jurors leave the courtroom, Glenn says that he is not surprised by the verdict. "I saw the writing on the wall. I don't think Joe was surprised either. The energy in the courtroom was against him.

"Maybe if I had done something differently," Glenn wonders aloud. "He's facing a lot of time."

The guards are about to take Joe Chen away. "Don't worry about me," he tells Glenn. "You did a good job."

Glenn says, "No matter what he may have done, Joe is still a human being. People can do terrible things, but they are still human beings. I fought for him and I care about him."

. . .

Leemie still can't believe that the trial is over. "I'm so relieved for my victims," she says over and over again. "They were so brave to come forward. I was so worried for them and their families." She begins to pack up her files. "I just want to stay in bed for days and days and days."

"All right, counsel," says Judge Fried. "Thank you. Have a good summer."

"Thank you," says Glenn. "You, too."

"Thank you, judge," says Leemie.

AFTERWORD

TIME: SEPTEMBER 28. 1998; 12:30 P.M.
PLACE: JUDGE FRIED'S COURTROOM

Judge Fried sentences Joe Chen to fifty years to life in prison. His case is currently on appeal.

NOTES

(Numbers refer to pages in text.)

5.   In China it is traditional for the family name to come first and the given name to follow. Here's how I chose the first two names:

Jiao Jin Hong, a law professor in China, helped me choose the victims' names. We chose "Wang" because it is a common name in China, similar to "Smith." I described the first victim as someone who was courageous, bold, and proud. He suggested the given name "Dong." It means "east."

I chose the family name of the second victim, Li, because Prince Li is one of my favorite characters in Chinese history. But then, when I described him as a follower of the first victim, Professor Jiao suggested that I use the name Jun which means "soldier." When the two names are pronounced together they sound like the English word "legion."

6.   The name of the informant Jane Ding was suggested by Wang Pei, another law professor in Beijing. She told me that the name "Ding" is similar to the way we use "Doe." Therefore, the informants are the Chinese equivalent to "Jane Doe" and "Johnny Doe." Notice that I have reversed the order of all the Chinese witnesses whose given names are anglicized.

6.   The Tung On is a ruthless Chinese street gang involved in such crimes as extortion, robbery, beatings, prostitution, smuggling, and

murder. They "work" in Chinatown around Division Street and East Broadway.

7.   At the request of the district attorney's office, all the locations outside New York City were changed.

14.   For history buffs, the Qin dynasty reigned from 221 to 207 B.C.

18.   This case was originally assigned to another assistant district attorney, but she went on maternity leave. Leemie is the second lawyer to work on the kidnapping.

24.   If you would like to look up this ruling, here is the citation: *People v. Rosario*, 9 N.Y. 2d 286 (1961).

New York Criminal Procedure Law Section 240.45: 1. After the jury has been sworn and before the prosecutor's opening address, or in the case of a single judge trial after commencement and before submission of evidence, the prosecutor shall, subject to a protective order, make available to the defendant:

a: Any written or recorded statement, including any testimony before a grand jury and an examination videotaped pursuant to section 190.32 of this chapter, made by a person whom the prosecutor intends to call as a witness at trial, and which relates to the subject matter of the witness's testimony.

78.   If you would like to look up this ruling, here is the citation: *People v. Bernard*, 637 N.Y. 2d 192 (N.Y. App. Div. 1996).

110.   I chose the name Echo because it is the English translation of a caring and helpful woman whom I met in Beijing. She reminded me of the "real" person who is about to take the witness stand.

114.   Some legal history: Lord Coke [pronounced Cook], 1552–1634, defines judicial discretion to be " *'discernere per legem quid sit justum,'* to see what would be just according to the laws in the premises.' It does not mean a wild self-willfulness, which may prompt any and every act; but this judicial discretion is guided by the law so as to do substantial equity and justice" (*Black's Law Dictionary*).

Catherine Drinker Bowen wrote a biography of Lord Coke called *The Lion and the Throne.* She describes his background. "Attorney General, Speaker of the House of Commons, Chief Justice of England, and the prime author, in 1628, of the great 'Petition of Right,' which served as a model for our Revolutionary forefathers."

125.   If you would like to look up this ruling, here is the citation: *People v. Sandoval,* 34 N.Y. 2d 371; 357 N.Y. 2d 849; 314 N.Y. 2d 413 (1974).

135.   Attenuation was described to me by Professor Susan Herman of Brooklyn Law School.

154.   Sequestering the jury: About three years before this trial, the New York State legislature enacted a law that gives the defendant the right to have the jurors isolated while they deliberate on serious criminal cases, such as murder or kidnapping.

During the trial Judge Fried asked Joe Chen if he would waive the right to sequester the jury. The defendant would not.

158.   Another piece of legal history: "In Roman law, *stipulatio* was the verbal contract (*verbis obligatio*) and was the most solemn and formal of all the contracts in that system of jurisprudence. It was entered into by the question and corresponding answer thereto, by the parties, both being present at the same time, and usually by such words as *Spondes? Spondeo, Promittis? Promitto*" (*Black's Law Dictionary*).

158.   Both summations are excerpted.

170.   After the verdict, Judge Fried met with the jurors privately to thank them for their hard work. A number of the jurors were curious about the lone person, me, who sat in the first row behind Joe Chen. The judge explained that I was writing this book. Although they had no obligation to discuss what took place during the deliberations, a handful of jurors said that they would like to talk to me.

From their reports, I was able to reconstruct part of their deliberation.

179.   Five sentencing principles guided Judge Fried's sentence:

1. One who commits a crime must suffer the consequences of his actions.

2. A punishment should be imposed to reduce the possibility of committing further crimes.

3. There is a need to protect society.

4. Rehabilitation of the person who commits the crime should be considered.

5. A loud and clear signal should be sent to the members of this community that criminal conduct will not be tolerated.

GLOSSARY

The following definitions are from *Black's Law Dictionary*, *Gilbert Law Dictionary*, and *Merriam-Webster's Collegiate Dictionary*.

ABDUCT. To restrict a person with the intent to prevent his release either by holding him in a place where he is not likely to be found or by using or threatening to use deadly physical force.

APPLICATION. A request or petition.

ARRAIGNMENT. The first step of a criminal proceeding where an accused person is brought before a judge and told of the charges against him or her.

CASE LAW. Law based on judicial precedent rather than legislative decrees; the body of law founded in decided cases rather than from statutes.

CHALLENGE. To object, to call into question, or to take exception. There are two types of challenges in jury selection, peremptory and challenge for cause. A *peremptory challenge* does not require that the attorney state a reason for an objection. A *challenge for cause* requires that the attorney state reasons for an objection.

COMPLAINT REPORT. An account that the police department uses to initiate an investigation.

CONCURRENT. Running together; for example, prison sentences that are served at the same time.

CONSECUTIVE. One after another; for example, prison sentences that are served one after another.

CONTINUANCE. An adjournment or postponement of a court action to a future time or date.

COUNT. A part of an indictment charging a specific offense.

DEADLY PHYSICAL FORCE. Physical force that is capable of causing death or other serious physical injury.

DEFENDANT. The person accused in a criminal case or sued in a civil action.

FELONY. A crime graver or more atrocious than one designated a misdemeanor and is punishable by imprisonment for more than one year.

HEARSAY. Evidence not proceeding from the personal knowledge of the witness but from the reiteration of another person's statement.

HOSTILE WITNESS. A witness who is adverse or antagonistic to the interests of the party that called him to testify.

INDICTMENT. An accusation by a grand jury. An indictment also serves to describe the specific charges so that the defendant may prepare an adequate defense.

INTENT. The design, resolve, or purpose with which a person acts.

IRRELEVANT. Not directly supporting the evidence of the case.

LARCENY. The unlawful taking of personal property with the intent to deprive the rightful owner of it permanently.

LARCENY BY EXTORTION. The unlawful taking of another's personal property by means of instilling fear that if the property is not delivered, the actor will cause physical injury to him or her sometime in the future.

MISDEMEANOR. A crime that is less serious than a felony and that is punishable by fine or imprisonment for less than one year.

MOTION. A formal request to the judge for a favorable order, ruling, or direction.

MOTIVE. The reason or influence that causes a person to act in a certain manner; contrasted with "intent," it is the purpose a person has when acting.

OFFER OF PROOF. The presentation of evidence for admission in a hearing or trial.

PENAL LAW. State and federal laws that define criminal offenses and create punishment of fines or imprisonment. A "penal code" is a collection of all the state's criminal laws.

PHYSICAL INJURY. Damage to one's physical condition or substantial pain.

PROBABLE CAUSE. The existence of certain facts that would lead a person of reasonable intelligence and prudence to believe a crime has been committed. Probable cause is required before an arrest or search warrant is issued by a judge.

RANSOM. Money or other property paid or demanded for the release of a captive person.

REDACT. Black out, edit.

RELEVANT. Evidence or testimony that tends to support an issue.

REVERSAL. An appellate court's changing or annulling a lower court's decision.

SEALED. Closed against inspection.

SEQUESTER. Hold apart, isolate.

SERIOUS PHYSICAL INJURY. An injury that causes death, brings about the substantial risk of death, or causes disfigurement, impairment of health, or loss or damage of the function of any bodily organ.

SIDEBAR. An on-the-record conversation away from the hearing of the jury. These discussions are recorded for purposes of an appeal.

STATUTE. A law established by the legislature.

SUBPOENA. A judicial order requiring a person to appear in court.

VOIR DIRE (FRENCH). To speak the truth. An examination of a prospective witness or juror to determine competency.

WELL. An area cordoned off from the public where the business of the court takes place.

FURTHER READING

There are so many interesting books about trials and about the law that it would be impossible to include all of them in this bibliography. Instead, Bernard J. Fried, Leemie Kahng, and I selected the following few books to share with you:

CAPOTE, TRUMAN. *In Cold Blood.* 1994. The re-creation of a 1959 murder in Kansas, including the investigation, capture, trial, and execution of the perpetrators.

ENGLISH, T. J. *Born to Kill: The Rise and Fall of America's Bloodiest Asian Gang.* 1996.

————. *The Westies: Inside Hell's Kitchen, Inside the Mob.* 1993.

GOODMAN, JAMES E. *Stories of Scottsboro.* 1995. The tale of nine black youths falsely accused and tried for the rape of two white women in 1931.

HARR, JOHNATHAN. *A Civil Action.* 1995. The fascinating true story of a civil trial.

KLUGER, RICHARD. *Simple Justice.* 1997. The history of *Brown v. Board of Education,* the case that ended segregation in the public schools.

LAWRENCE, JEROME, AND ROBERT E. LEE. *Inherit the Wind.* 1982. Darwin's theory of evolution is put on trial.

LEE, HARPER. *To Kill a Mockingbird.* 1999. A novel set in Alabama in which a white lawyer is appointed to defend a black defendant accused of rape.

LEWIS, ANTHONY. *Gideon's Trumpet.* 1989. A classic. Insight into the workings of the Supreme Court in granting protection to criminal defendants.

MAAS, PETER. *Serpico.* 1997. The story of Frank Serpico, a police officer who exposed bad cops.

MELVILLE, HERMAN. *Billy Budd.* 1998. A novel about an envious man whose conduct leads to a trial for treason of a handsome sailor.

TRAVER, ROBERT. *Anatomy of a Murder.* 1983. Another courtroom classic novel.

TUROW, SCOTT. *One L: The Turbulent True Story of a First Year at Harvard Law School.* 1997.

WELLMAN, FRANCIS L. *The Art of Cross Examination.* 1998. Techniques for different kinds of cross-examinations.

The following are young-adult books that deal with criminal trials and legal issues (with many thanks to Eliza Dresang for helping to research this list):

BODE, JANET, AND STAN MACK. *Hard Time: A Real Life Look at Juvenile Crime and Violence.* 1996.

MYERS, WALTER DEAN. *Monster.* 1999. A sixteen-year-old is on trial for murder in this novel.

————. *Amistad: A Long Road to Freedom.* 1998.

NICHOLS, JOAN KANE. *A Matter of Conscience: The Trial of Anne Hutchinson.* 1993.

NUNEZ, SANDRA JOSEPH, AND TRISH NUNEZ. *And Justice for All: The Legal Rights of Young People.* 1997. An ACLU handbook for young Americans.

PASCOE, ELAINE. *America's Courts on Trial: Questioning Our Legal System.* 1997.

RAPP, ADAM. *The Buffalo Tree.* 1997. A novel set inside a juvenile detention center.

INDEX

(Page numbers in *italic* refer to illustrations.)